healthy food

Lesley Waters

photography by Gus Filgate

ALHAMBRA
EDITIONS

This edition first published in 2007 by **Alhambra editions**
Alhambra House, 27-31 Charing Cross Road, London WC2H 0LS

This edition printed exclusively for The Works

Editorial director Jane O'Shea
Creative director Helen Lewis
Managing editor Janet Illsley
Art direction Vanessa Courtier
Design Ros Holder and Amanda Lerwill
Photographer Gus Filgate
Food stylist Silvana Franco
Props stylist Jane Campsie
Editor Barbara Croxford
Production Ruth Deary

Text © 2003 Lesley Waters **Photography** © 2003 Gus Filgate
Design and layout © 2005 Quadrille Publishing Limited

Originally published exclusively for J Sainsbury plc.

Cataloguing in Publication Data: a catalogue record for this book is available
from the British Library.

ISBN: 978 184400 471 3

Printed in China

Cookery notes
All spoon measures are level: 1 tsp = 5ml spoon; 1 tbsp = 15ml spoon.
Use fresh herbs and freshly ground black pepper unless otherwise suggested.
Free-range eggs are recommended and large eggs should be used except
where a different size is specified. Recipes with raw or lightly cooked eggs
should be avoided by anyone who is pregnant or in a vulnerable health group.

Contents

Introduction

Whether I am working on television, teaching or writing, I am often asked if it is really possible to deliver simple, tasty, healthy food every day, with the minimum of effort. And my answer is yes, because for me this is what good food is all about. Healthy eating is not a fad, it's not a diet, nor is it something you practise for two weeks before your summer holiday. It's a great way to live and enjoy your food. And that, quite simply, is what this book is all about.

Most of us lead busy lives and time is precious. Finding the time to shop, cook and eat three meals a day without resorting to quick fixes can seem impossible at times, but it can be done. Once hooked on a healthy diet, you will never look back and you will reap the benefits. I believe it is the simple changes that make the difference. It's not about giving up everything that is tasty and good to eat, just about making adjustments.

The key to healthy eating is about making changes that easily become part of your everyday life. One adjustment you can make is to invest in great fresh produce. Ask any top chef and he or she will tell you that to create tasty, simple food, quality is everything. Consider free-range and organic foods, and when it comes to fish and meat I look for the best quality possible, always bearing in mind that less is more and quality counts.

Enjoying your food in the company of others is a great way to socialise with family and friends, and helps children form good eating habits. However hectic your day is, do try to sit down to at least one meal with the family. Take the time to eat slowly and chew your food properly – this makes it easier to digest, and easier for your body to absorb the nutrients. Avoid overeating – recognise when you are full, then stop. Try not to skip meals and you will really look forward to and enjoy the next meal.

This book begins with an introduction to the basic principles, or 'building blocks', that are essential to a good diet. It covers balanced nutrition, judicious shopping, useful equipment, healthy cooking methods and food safety. The recipe chapters that follow provide a wealth of exciting, tasty dishes, based on fresh ingredients and uncomplicated cooking techniques, together with healthy diet tips. Every meal occasion is covered, from breakfast, through lunchboxes, tasty snacks, suppers and dinners. Scrumptious puddings are included too, because healthy eating is about a balanced approach to food, not excluding those foods that you enjoy.

With this innovative easy-to-follow cookbook, you will soon find that healthy eating becomes a positive pleasure.

Building blocks

Eating a variety of foods is the key to a nutritious, healthy diet. It's also important to balance your intake. The best diet includes plenty of fresh ingredients, covering the whole range of food types, to ensure your body gets enough of the essential nutrients: proteins, vitamins, minerals, carbohydrates and fats. Some foods are obviously better for you than others.

Hydration

Our bodies are made up of approximately 80 per cent water, so top of my list has to be water. Although it isn't a nutrient, water is vital for so many of our bodily functions. Ideally, we should consume around 2 litres (3½ pints) water a day. That is equivalent to a big bottle of still mineral water or 8 large glasses a day. For many of us, this is difficult to achieve, but other drinks help towards that target (excluding alcohol), and remember that many fruit and vegetables contain lots of water, so it all adds up. Tea and coffee both have a diuretic effect, encouraging the body to eliminate water, so they should be consumed in moderation. Always provide water with meals, and try to remember to drink at least a large glass or two in between meals.

Five-a-day fruit and veg

This is the recommended number of portions that we should consume every day. Fruit and vegetables are valuable because they supply the body's defence system with the vitamins, minerals and fibre it needs to keep in good health. 'Five-a-day' may seem a lot, but dried fruits and fruit juices count too.

Most vegetables and fruits are virtually fat-free, high in fibre and contain antioxidants. These boost the immune system and may help to protect the body from diseases, including some forms of cancer. Tomatoes, red peppers, mangoes and avocados are particularly high in antioxidants. Vegetables and fruits vary in the essential nutrients that they provide, so you need to eat a good variety for maximum benefit. Fresh vegetables can be cooked in so many interesting ways, or eaten raw in salads or as crudités for dipping. Beyond the fruit bowl, enjoy quick smoothies, fruit salads, salsas, hot fruity puddings, and dried fruit as snacks. Buy good quality fruit juice, or if you have a juicer, make your own delicious vegetable and fruit juices.

Protein foods

We need far less protein than most of us consume – as little as 75g (3oz) a day is generally sufficient. Again, variety is the key. White meat is a good source of protein and it has less saturated fat than red meat, although you can now buy very lean cuts of red meat. Fish is an excellent source of protein, especially oily fish such as salmon, mackerel and sardines. And don't forget beans and lentils, nuts and seeds, which provide valuable vitamins and minerals too. Lastly, there is the versatile egg, a concentrated source of animal protein.

Salt

On average in this country, we consume about 1½ times more salt than is recommended. Too much salt can contribute to high blood pressure and has been linked to coronary heart disease, so it makes sense to cut down on your salt intake. These days, I do not use salt in my cooking. If you wish to add salt to some of these recipes, that's fine, but try to cut down gradually. Perhaps the first step is to stop adding it during cooking. When you are accustomed to the new taste, banish the salt pot from the table. It is amazing how quickly your tastebuds adjust and you find you prefer less salt.

Sugar

Refined sugars provide 'empty calories' and, if eaten frequently, increase the risk of tooth decay, so we should aim to cut down on these. Apart from the obvious sources, like sweets, biscuits and cakes, watch out for hidden sugars in processed foods, such as sweetened breakfast cereals. Try to buy 'no added sugar' breakfast cereals and sweeten with naturally sweet fresh and dried fruits – raisins and fresh banana slices on muesli, for example.

Soft drinks, in particular, can contain large quantities of added sugar. Choose fresh fruit juices without added sugar, and look for lower sugar options if you buy fruit squashes.

Fats

In general, we consume too much fat. A small amount of fat plays a role in the overall balance of a healthy diet, but eating too much is harmful. Fats are composed of fatty acids, and it is the saturated type found in meat, dairy products and hard cooking fats that are particularly harmful.

A high intake of saturated fatty acids is linked to an increased risk of heart disease, obesity and certain forms of cancer. To cut down, avoid dripping and lard, and be wary of the hidden fats in bought biscuits, cakes, pastries and some ready meals. Opt for lean cuts of meat and smaller portions, topping up your plate with plenty of vegetables. Choose very strong cheese to use in cooking, such as Parmesan, because you'll need only a small amount to impart flavour. And butter? Well it makes sense to cut down, but I prefer a fine scraping of butter on toast to any low-fat spread. It's all a question of awareness and a balanced approach.

Monounsaturated fatty acids are found in foods such as olive oil, sesame and rapeseed oils, avocados, seeds and most nuts. These are not detrimental to health provided they are consumed in moderation (to avoid weight gain), and they can help to lower the potentially harmful type of cholesterol in blood.

Polyunsaturated fatty acids include the essential omega-3 and omega-6 fatty acids that are important for growth, a healthy skin and a strong immune system. Oily fish, soya beans and rapeseed oil are good sources of omega-3's; vegetable oils, such as sunflower and olive oil, contain omega-6's. These are beneficial sources of fat.

Hydrogenated fats are found in cooking fats, margarines, pastries and processed ready meals. These contain trans fatty acids, which work like saturated fats. It is therefore preferable to avoid these or limit your intake in the same way as saturated fats.

Fibre
This isn't a nutrient as such, but it is an important constituent of food, which helps to keep the digestive system healthy. Wholemeal bread, wholegrain cereals, fruit, vegetables, pulses and nuts are good sources.

My top ten 'super foods'

Some foods are so nutritious, you could almost call them 'super foods'. These foods contain beneficial oils and/or high levels of antioxidants in the form of beta-carotene and vitamins C and E, all of which contribute to helping to reduce the risk of serious diseases, such as heart disease and certain forms of cancer. Eat them regularly to maximise the benefits to your diet. Many foods could be described as 'super foods', but these are my ten favourites.

Avocado This fruit is rich in beneficial monounsaturated fatty acids, contains more protein than any other fruit, and is an excellent source of vitamin E.

Bananas An excellent instant energy food and easy to digest, bananas are also high in potassium, magnesium and some B vitamins.

Berries Blackcurrants, blueberries, blackberries and black grapes are all high in antioxidants.

Green vegetables Brassicas, such as broccoli, Brussels sprouts, cabbage and greens, contain beneficial phytochemicals called indoles, which can help to detoxify the body if eaten regularly. They are also useful sources of minerals.

Oats Whole oats are an excellent source of soluble fibre and a slow-release form of carbohydrate. They can also help to maintain a healthy heart.

Oily fish All varieties are good sources of protein and rich in beneficial omega-3 fatty acids, minerals and certain vitamins.

Red and yellow peppers Rich in beta-carotene and vitamin C.

Seeds Sesame, pumpkin and sunflower seeds are packed with protein, high in essential oils, and a valuable source of vitamin E and B vitamins.

Soya An important high quality vegetable protein food, especially for vegetarians, and a good source of minerals, B vitamins and antioxidants. Soya is available as bean curd (tofu), soya milk, cheese and yogurts.

Tomatoes Another colourful food that is rich in beta-carotene and a good source of vitamins C and E.

'Storecupboard' essentials

Certain ingredients have become the jewels of my kitchen cupboards, fridge and freezer. These items ensure that tasty, healthy food is achievable every single day and I would be lost without them. In addition, I always have a huge bowl of apples, pears, oranges, lemons and limes on the kitchen table, and a bunch of bananas in a separate bowl.

Kitchen cupboards I keep a selection of the basic grain staples such as pasta, cous cous, cracked wheat, polenta and different rices, plus different coloured lentils, canned beans and tomatoes, and packets of nuts and seeds. For flavouring dishes, my storecupboard jewels are: Thai curry pastes, half-fat coconut milk, wine and balsamic vinegars, soy, teriyaki, Tabasco and Worcestershire sauces, Dijon and wholegrain mustards, chilli flakes and a selection of spices including ground coriander, sweet paprika and garam masala. If you are trying to cut down on salt, these flavourings – together with fresh herbs, ginger and garlic – will give you all the taste you need. You'll also need good quality olive oil to use in moderation for cooking and salad dressings. And for flavouring sweet dishes, you'll find honey, maple syrup and vanilla extract invaluable.

Refrigerator There is always fresh fruit juice, milk, yogurt, eggs, a piece of strong Cheddar cheese and a wedge of Parmesan in my fridge. Lean back bacon, olive tapenade, sun-blushed tomatoes, tahini and fresh ready-made pesto are there to add flavour to simple staples. In the vegetable drawer, you'll find nutritious broccoli, carrots, peppers and baby spinach leaves. The salad drawer invariably contains a bag of salad leaves, ripe red tomatoes, cucumber and a selection of chillies for easy raitas and spicy salsas.

Freezer I have never been inclined to cook up meals for the freezer. They lose some qualities on freezing and I prefer to eat dishes at their best. However, I would not be without my freezer-standbys, such as sweetcorn, peas and spinach, red summer fruits and frozen yogurts. A few pitta breads and good quality loaves are always handy for those occasions when you run short.

Key cooking methods

Modern cooking equipment greatly increases the options for healthy cooking techniques. Good quality non-stick pans enable you to cook tasty dishes using the minimum of oil or fat. They are important for many of the recipes in this book and essential for methods such as steam-frying. If you do not have them already, invest in a large non-stick wok with a lid, a non-stick frying pan with a lid, one or two non-stick saucepans and non-stick roasting tins in two different sizes. For baking, non-stick muffins tins and good quality non-stick baking trays and baking sheets are most useful.

Steaming

Steaming is a classic cooking method for healthy food. Chinese bamboo steamers are an attractive option that can be used for serving the food as well as cooking it. Alternatively, try a metal fan style steamer that opens out to fit the pan, or a special purpose pan with a perforated steamer that fits snugly on top. A tight-fitting lid is essential to trap in the steam. Bring the water to the boil in the base of the pan, then put the food in the steamer and cover tightly. The food cooks in the trapped steam and water-soluble vitamins and minerals are retained. You will need to check the water level every so often, to make sure the pan doesn't boil dry.

Poaching

Poaching is an ideal way to cook delicate foods that are inclined to break easily, such as eggs and fish. Bring the liquid to the boil in the pan, then lower the heat and wait until the surface is barely trembling before you add the food. Poaching is also a good method for foods that are liable to become dry. Chicken breasts, for example, remain succulent if you poach them gently in stock or wine flavoured with herbs and you can reduce the poaching liquor to make a tasty sauce.

Griddling

Traditional cast-iron griddle pans are good for cooking steaks and chops, but otherwise their use is limited and they are heavy to handle. The modern, lightweight, non-stick griddle pan is ideal for cooking meat, fish, vegetables and fruits, even for toasting bread. Griddling is like upside-down grilling, as the heat of the pan sears the food on the outside giving it an inviting appearance, taste and texture, with the added advantage that very little fat is needed. Make sure the griddle pan is really hot before you start. If you need a little oil, this should be brushed on to the food, not the pan. Press down on the food with the back of a fish slice as it cooks to give defined char-grill lines, but don't move it around too much.

Stir-frying

The oriental art of stir-frying is a fast, healthy way of cooking food and nutrients are well retained. Once again you need to start with a hot pan, but this time when the food is added, you need to keep it moving to ensure even cooking. Have all your ingredients ready chopped or sliced to a similar size before you start – once you start you can't stop! Make sure the wok is really hot before you add any ingredients and avoid adding too many items in one go, otherwise you will lower the temperature. Use a large spoon, wooden spatula or fish slice to toss and stir the food constantly.

Steam-frying

I learnt this brilliant way of cooking from a good friend. It is a simple technique that uses the minimum amount of oil, while maximising the flavours in the food. Using a non-stick pan, start to fry the ingredient(s) in a little oil over a medium heat until slightly coloured. Add a tablespoon or so of water and cover immediately with a tight-fitting lid to create steam in the pan. Continue to cook over a low heat. If your lid isn't really tight, cover the food directly with a damp piece of greaseproof paper or baking parchment, then with a lid. Don't keep lifting the lid, as steam will be lost and the pan will dry out. Should this happen, just add a splash more water.

Grilling

Meat, fish and vegetables can all benefit from grilling as it sears the outside of the food, leaving it juicy and succulent within. Preheat the grill to the correct temperature, and keep a close eye on the food as it grills, turning frequently to ensure even cooking. If it appears to be browning too quickly, either move the shelf down or lower the heat.

Oven roasting

This familiar method requires the least effort on the part of the cook. Simply preheat the oven to the right temperature, toss the foods in a roasting tin with a little oil or marinade and place in the oven. The dry heat draws out the juices from the food, concentrating the flavours and caramelising the surface to delicious effect. You'll need to turn or baste the food occasionally during roasting, remembering to shut the oven door as you do so, to keep the oven temperature up. Even vegetables need tossing during roasting.

healthy breakfasts, snacks and lunchboxes

Balsamic tomatoes with crispy ham

Serves 4
4 beefsteak tomatoes, halved
1 tsp dried chilli flakes
1 tsp caster sugar
1½ tbsp olive oil

70g packet Parma or Black Forest
 ham
balsamic vinegar, to drizzle
freshly ground black pepper
basil leaves, to serve (optional)

1 Preheat the oven to 200°C (fan oven 180°C), gas mark 6. Preheat the grill. Place the tomatoes, cut-side up, on a non-stick baking tray. Mix together the chilli, sugar and olive oil, then drizzle over the tomato halves. Grind over plenty of black pepper. Bake for 12–15 minutes until the tomatoes are cooked through but still keeping their shape.
2 Meanwhile, grill the ham for 1 minute each side or until crispy. Place the tomatoes on four warm serving plates, then drizzle each with a little balsamic vinegar. Top with the crispy ham, scatter with basil leaves if you like and serve, with Granary toast.

Breakfast with a zing – sizzling tomatoes with a chilli kick and balsamic vinegar. Tomatoes are a great source of vitamins A and C. If you don't fancy chilli, scatter the tomatoes with a little shredded fresh basil instead.

Steam-fried eggs

Serves 4
a little olive oil
4 eggs
handful of small basil leaves
freshly ground black pepper
4 slices of wholemeal bread, toasted

1 Heat a large non-stick frying pan until very hot, then carefully wipe with kitchen paper dipped in oil.
2 Crack the eggs into the pan, spacing them apart, and reduce the heat to low. Cover with a lid, so they start to steam, and cook for about 4 minutes for soft eggs, or flip over for a minute if you prefer a firm set yolk.
3 Season with black pepper and scatter over a little basil. Serve on toast.

A healthy fried egg, cooked in the minimum of oil, makes a tasty, nourishing breakfast that will keep you sustained through to lunch.

Posh porridge

Serves 4
225g (8oz) jumbo oats
300ml (½ pint) semi-skimmed milk
100g (3½oz) natural bio yogurt
100ml (3½oz) blueberries
a little maple syrup, to drizzle

1 Make the porridge with the jumbo oats according to the packet
instructions, using the semi-skimmed milk and an equal amount of water
(or as directed).
2 Top with a spoonful of natural bio yogurt, the blueberries and a drizzle of
maple syrup. Serve at once.

There's nothing like porridge oats to set you
up for the day. They are a good source of
'slow-release' energy, help reduce cholesterol
and they encourage the digestive system to
run smoothly.

Oaty orange and fig pots

Serves 2

125g (4oz) large oats

4 dried figs, roughly chopped, or a generous handful of sultanas or raisins

300ml (½ pint) orange juice

To serve

Greek yogurt

toasted flaked almonds (optional)

1 Divide the oats and dried fruit between two serving bowls and pour over the orange juice. Cover and chill for 4 hours or overnight.

2 To serve, top each portion with a spoonful of yogurt and sprinkle with toasted almonds if you like.

Here orange juice and chopped figs provide an added bonus of vitamin C and fibre to a healthy oat breakfast.

Toasted breakfast wraps

Illustrated on previous pages

Serves 4
2 large bananas
2 nectarines, halved and stoned
2 tsp thin honey
4 flour tortillas

1 Chop the bananas and nectarines and toss with the honey. Spoon the fruit down the centre of the tortillas and roll up, folding in the ends to enclose and form wraps.
2 Heat a non-stick griddle pan over a medium heat. Place the tortilla wraps, seam-side down, in the pan and cook for 2 minutes each side. Serve warm.

As a variation, fill the tortillas with scrambled eggs flavoured with halved cherry tomatoes and slivers of honey roast ham.

Tea-scented warm fruits

Serves 4
150g (5oz) dried figs
150g (5oz) ready-to-eat dried prunes
150g (5oz) dried pears
2 lemon green tea bags
1 tbsp thin honey

1 Put the dried figs, prunes and pears into a saucepan. Add the tea bags, 600ml (1 pint) water and the honey. Bring to the boil, lower the heat and simmer for 10 minutes.
2 Remove the tea bags and tip the fruits and syrup into a non-metallic bowl. Serve warm, or set aside to cool then cover and refrigerate until needed.

This fruit compote is good with hot porridge, breakfast wheat flakes or simply on its own. As well as being full of fibre, dried fruits are a good source of iron. Other varieties can be substituted, such as dried apricots.

Apricot and maple muffins

Illustrated on previous pages

Makes 8–10
2 eggs
250ml (8fl oz) semi-skimmed milk
2 tbsp olive oil
3 tbsp natural yogurt
50g (2oz) All-bran
225g (8oz) plain white flour
1 tbsp baking powder
25g (1oz) light muscovado sugar
125g (4oz) ready-to-eat dried
   apricots, chopped
50g (2oz) sultanas
2 tbsp maple syrup

1 Preheat the oven to 190°C (fan oven 170°C), gas mark 5. Line a large muffin tin with 8–10 paper cases or greaseproof paper. In a measuring jug, mix together the eggs, milk, olive oil, yogurt and bran. Set aside.
2 Sift the flour and baking powder into a bowl, then stir in the sugar, dried apricots and sultanas. Add the egg mixture and mix well until smooth. Spoon the mixture into the muffin cases.
3 Bake for 15–20 minutes until golden and cooked through. Insert a skewer into the middle of one muffin to test – when cooked, the skewer will come out clean. Remove from the oven.
4 Allow the muffins to cool in the tin for a few minutes, then transfer to a wire rack and brush with the maple syrup. Serve warm or allow to cool.

Even with added fibre-rich bran, these fruity muffins remain beautifully moist. They are flavoured with dried apricots, one of the best sources of iron and potassium, and sweetened with maple syrup. Great for breakfast on the go, or lunchboxes.

Banana breakfast bread

Makes 9 large buns
290g packet pizza dough mix
3 medium bananas, peeled
grated zest of 1 orange
1 tbsp poppy seeds
½ tsp ground cinnamon
1½ tbsp thin honey

1 Preheat the oven to 200°C (fan oven 180°C), gas mark 6. Lightly oil a 20cm (8 inch) square non-stick baking tin. Make up the dough mix according to the packet instructions. Roll out to a rectangle, approximately 30 x 25cm (12 x 10 inches).
2 Slice the bananas and place in a bowl with the orange zest, poppy seeds, cinnamon and half of the honey. Toss to mix, then spoon the mixture over the dough, leaving a 1cm (½ inch) border.
3 Roll up the dough from a long side and press the edges together to seal. Cut into nine equal pieces and place the dough pieces, cut-side up, in the tin.
4 Bake for 15–20 minutes. Warm the remaining honey in the microwave for 5 seconds (or in a small pan) and brush over the breakfast bread. Leave in the tin to cool slightly, then remove. Pull the buns apart to serve – they are best eaten warm.

A simple, quick bread oozing with hot honeyed bananas. Bananas are a good source of energy, vitamin B6, which is said to fight off viruses, plus vitamin C and magnesium.

Breakfast blinis

Serves 4

125g (4oz) self-raising flour
½ tsp ground cinnamon
15g (½oz) caster sugar
grated zest of 1 orange

50g (2oz) sultanas
1 egg
200ml (7fl oz) milk
50g (2oz) bran flakes, crumbled
a little olive oil

1 Sift the flour and cinnamon together into a bowl. Stir in the sugar, grated orange zest and sultanas, then make a well in the centre.
2 Beat the egg with the milk, then pour into the well. Stir to combine and form a smooth batter. Stir in the crumbled bran flakes.
3 Heat a large non-stick frying pan, then wipe with kitchen paper dipped in olive oil. Drop tablespoonfuls of the batter into the pan, spacing them well apart to allow room for spreading. Cook for 2 minutes until set and golden underneath, then turn with a palette knife and cook for a further 2 minutes.
4 Serve warm, with yogurt or fruit if you like.

Don't skip breakfast at weekends. These tasty blinis are easy to make – perfect for brunch for late-risers.

Mango and banana smoothie

Serves 2–4
1 large ripe banana, peeled and
   roughly chopped
1 large ripe mango, peeled, stoned
   and sliced
grated zest and juice of 1 lime
200ml (7fl oz) orange juice, or more
   to taste

1 Place the banana, mango, lime zest and juice, and orange juice in a
blender. Blend until smooth, adding more orange juice if required to obtain
the desired consistency. Pour into two large glasses or several smaller ones
and serve straightaway.

A healthy drink is a great way to increase
your fruit and fibre intake at the flick of a
switch! The fruit must be really ripe, to ensure
the right consistency and natural sweetness.

Pineapple and passion slush

Serves 4
430g can pineapple slices, in natural
  juice
300g (11oz) natural bio fat-free
  yogurt
1 passion fruit, halved

1 Place the pineapple slices and juice in a blender with the yogurt. Put
10 ice cubes into a plastic bag and bash with a rolling pin to crush lightly.
Tip the ice into the blender and whiz until frothy and just smooth. Pour the
drink into four glasses and spoon a little passion fruit pulp on top to serve.

Creamy and refreshing in one hit – a great
start to the morning, or to enjoy at any time
as one of your five-a-day fruit and veg. Be
sure to buy pineapple canned in its own juice.

Pink panther

Serves 2–4

175g (6oz) mixed strawberries and
   raspberries
150ml (¼ pint) cranberry juice
225g (8oz) low-fat vanilla yogurt

1 Place the strawberries, raspberries, cranberry juice and vanilla yogurt in a blender and whiz until smooth. Fill two large glasses or several smaller tumblers with crushed ice and pour the smoothie on top to serve.

This delicious drink provides a real burst of energy in a glass and boosts your vitamin C intake. For a summer cooler, replace the vanilla yogurt with frozen vanilla yogurt.

Mango and carrot crumble cookies

Illustrated on previous pages

Makes 16

50g (2oz) butter
65g (2½oz) dark muscovado sugar
1 egg
50g (2oz) plain flour
½ tsp bicarbonate of soda
150g (5oz) porridge oats
1 small carrot, peeled and grated
65g (2½oz) dried mango, finely
    chopped

1 Preheat the oven to 190°C (fan oven 170°C), gas mark 5. In a large bowl, cream the butter and sugar together. Add the egg and beat until well mixed.
2 Sift the flour and bicarbonate of soda together over the mixture, then add the porridge oats, grated carrot and chopped mango. Fold in, using a large metal spoon, until evenly mixed.
3 Drop tablespoons of the dough on to a non-stick baking sheet and press down gently with the back of a fork. Bake for 15–20 minutes or until lightly golden around the edges.
4 Leave the cookies on the baking sheet for a few minutes, then transfer to a wire rack to cool.

Crumbly around the edges and moist in the middle, these cookies are a favourite with children. The grated carrot and dried mango lend sweetness and plenty of goodness. Oats provide crunch and soluble fibre.

Chunky pear and vanilla flapjacks

Makes 10

7 tbsp thin honey

3 tsp vanilla extract

150g (5oz) porridge oats

75g (3oz) dried cranberries

2 medium ripe pears, peeled, cored
and chopped

1 Preheat the oven to 180°C (fan oven 160°C), gas mark 4. Heat the honey in a saucepan, add the vanilla, then stir in the oats, cranberries and pears.

2 Press the mixture into an 18cm (7 inch) square non-stick baking tin and bake for 20 minutes. Leave to cool in the tin for 10 minutes, then mark into 10 bars and leave to cool completely before removing.

These crumbly, fruity flapjacks are high in fibre and low in fat. Packed with cranberries and pears, they make a great lunchbox filler, or snack at any time of the day.

Sultana and cranberry rockies

Makes 8

25g (1oz) unsalted butter
125g (4oz) self-raising flour
40g (1½oz) muscovado sugar
25g (1oz) sultanas
25g (1oz) dried cranberries
1 egg, beaten
1 tbsp milk

1 Preheat the oven to 180°C (fan oven 160°C), gas mark 4. Lightly oil a non-stick baking sheet. Put the butter and flour into a mixing bowl and rub together with your fingertips until the mixture resembles fine breadcrumbs. Stir in the sugar, sultanas and cranberries. Mix in the egg and milk to form a soft dough.
2 Drop spoonfuls of the mixture on to the baking sheet, spacing out well. Bake for 12–15 minutes until golden. Transfer to a wire rack to cool.

These quick and easy, sustaining treats are best eaten on the day they are made. Dried cranberries lend a tangy, sweet flavour.

Butter bean houmous

Serves 4

400g can butter beans, drained and
  rinsed
400g can chick peas, drained and
  rinsed
2 garlic cloves, peeled and crushed

2 tbsp tahini
3 tbsp extra virgin olive oil
3 tbsp natural yogurt
juice of ½ lemon
sea salt and pepper

1 Put the butter beans, chick peas, garlic, tahini, olive oil, yogurt and lemon juice in a food processor and add about 5 tbsp cold water. Whiz briefly until just smooth.

2 Season the houmous with a little sea salt and pepper to taste. Transfer to a bowl or plastic tub and serve with vegetable dippers and pitta bread strips.

This creamy, protein-rich houmous is very easy to make. Provide a colourful selection of vegetables for dipping, such as carrot and celery sticks, cherry tomatoes, crunchy radishes and little lettuce hearts.

Tuna pan bagna

Makes 4

4 ciabatta rolls
6 tbsp natural yogurt
1 garlic clove, peeled and crushed
1 tsp lemon juice
100g (3½oz) sun-blushed tomatoes

50g (2oz) crisp salad leaves
2 x 160g cans yellow fin tuna in
  spring water, drained
1 punnet mustard and cress,
  trimmed
freshly ground black pepper

1 Cut the top off each roll to make a lid. Hollow out the centre of the rolls.
(Use the scooped-out bread to make breadcrumbs and freeze for another use.)
2 To make the dressing, whisk the yogurt, garlic and lemon juice together
in a bowl, then season with pepper to taste.
3 Spoon the sun-blushed tomatoes into the ciabatta cavities and cover with a
layer of salad leaves. Spoon on some of the yogurt dressing, then add the
tuna, more dressing and a final layer of mustard and cress, pressing down
lightly as you fill the rolls.
4 Place the lids on top to enclose the filling and press lightly. Wrap the rolls
in greaseproof paper and refrigerate or keep in a chilled insulated lunchbox
for a few hours before eating (no longer or they may become a little soggy).

This is a crusty roll filled to the brim with
juicy semi-dried tomatoes, crispy leaves, tuna
and a creamy dressing. Canned tuna is high
in protein and vitamins, but unfortunately
most of the omega-3 essential fatty acids are
lost in the canning process.

Pesto picnic pasta

Serves 4–6

200g (7oz) dried pasta shapes, such
  as penne or shells
3 tbsp ready-made fresh pesto sauce
2 tbsp extra virgin olive oil
150g (5oz) cooked chicken breast,
  shredded

250g (9oz) vine-ripened cherry
  tomatoes, halved
1 cucumber, peeled, deseeded and
  chopped
freshly ground black pepper

1 Cook the pasta in a large pan of boiling water, according to the packet instructions, until al dente (tender, but firm to the bite). Drain and rinse under cold water to stop further cooking, then place in a large bowl and set aside to cool completely.

2 Meanwhile, for the dressing, whisk the pesto and olive oil together in a large mixing bowl. Season with pepper to taste.

3 Add the pasta, chicken, tomatoes and cucumber to the pesto dressing and toss well together. Transfer the pasta salad to a lidded container and refrigerate or keep in a chilled lunchbox until needed.

This nutritious salad is ideal to pack into tubs for lunchboxes. The pasta soaks up the flavour of the basil pesto and marries well with tender chicken, juicy tomatoes and cucumber.

healthy
soups

Green macaroni minestrone

Serves 4

150ml (¼ pint) white wine
1 onion, peeled and finely chopped
1 garlic clove, peeled and crushed
1.5 litres (2½ pints) vegetable stock
100g (3½oz) dried macaroni
125g (4oz) French beans, trimmed
  and cut into 2.5cm (1 inch)
  lengths

400g can cannellini beans, drained
  and rinsed
75g (3oz) frozen petit pois
2 ripe tomatoes, chopped
3 tbsp chopped basil
freshly ground black pepper
4 tsp extra virgin olive oil, to serve

1 Pour the white wine into a large pan and add the onion and garlic. Cover the pan and steam-fry for 6 minutes or until softened, stirring occasionally.
2 Add the stock and bring to the boil. Tip in the macaroni and cook for 6 minutes. Stir in the French beans and simmer for 3 minutes, then add the cannellini beans and petit pois and simmer for a further 2 minutes.
3 Add the tomatoes and basil, and heat through for 1 minute. Season well with pepper. Ladle the minestrone into four warm bowls and drizzle each with 1 tsp of extra virgin olive oil to serve.

A twist on the classic minestrone, this fresh-tasting soup is full of vegetables, rich in fibre and very satisfying – a real meal in itself. Serve with good crusty bread.

Veggie barley broth with garlic toasts

Illustrated on previous pages

Serves 4

1.5 litres (2½ pints) chicken or
  vegetable stock
100g (3½oz) pearl barley
1 leek, trimmed
2 celery sticks
2 large carrots, peeled
1 medium parsnip, peeled

5 tbsp white wine
2 tbsp sun-dried tomato paste
2 bay leaves
2 tbsp chopped parsley
freshly ground black pepper
For the garlic toasts
1 rustic loaf, sliced
1 garlic clove, peeled and halved

1 Pour the stock into a pan, add the pearl barley and boil gently for
10 minutes. Meanwhile, finely chop the leek, celery, carrots and parsnip.
2 Pour the wine into a large pan, add the leek, cover and steam-fry for
5 minutes, stirring occasionally. Add the remaining vegetables and cook for
a further 5 minutes.
3 Stir in the tomato paste, bay leaves, pearl barley and stock. Bring to the
boil, lower the heat and simmer for 15–20 minutes.
4 Meanwhile, toast the bread on both sides, then rub with the garlic clove.
Season the soup with pepper to taste and stir in the parsley. Pour into warm
bowls and serve with the garlic toasts.

This hearty root vegetable broth is full of fibre, which helps the body to absorb nutrients. It is thickened with pearl barley, which is an under-rated grain. It has a nutty flavour and lends a creamy texture to soups and stews.

Spiced red lentil and sweet potato soup

Serves 4

350g (12oz) potatoes
1 large sweet potato
2 tbsp ready-made curry paste, such as Madras or korma
1 onion, peeled and finely chopped
125g (4oz) split red lentils

900ml (1½ pints) vegetable stock
200ml (7fl oz) reduced-fat coconut milk
1–2 tbsp chopped coriander leaves, plus sprigs to garnish
freshly ground black pepper

1 Peel the potatoes and sweet potato and cut into 1cm (½ inch) cubes. Heat the curry paste in a pan, stir in the onion, cover and steam-fry for 5 minutes, stirring occasionally.

2 Add the potatoes, sweet potato, lentils and stock to the pan. Bring to the boil, then lower the heat and simmer for 20 minutes.

3 Stir in the coconut milk and gently heat through. Season to taste with pepper, then stir in the chopped coriander. Ladle the soup into warm bowls, top with coriander sprigs and serve with warm chapatti breads.

Lentils are full of fibre, which aids digestion, and they are a good source of vegetable protein. Serve this soup with warm chapatti bread as a lunch or light supper.

Pea and basil soup with tomato bruschetta

Serves 4

1 onion, peeled and chopped
1 tsp olive oil
1 litre (1¾ pints) vegetable stock
500g (1lb 2oz) petit pois
3 tbsp ready-made fresh pesto
freshly cracked black pepper

For the tomato bruschetta

4 thick slices of ciabatta
1 garlic clove, peeled and halved
4 large, ripe, flavourful tomatoes,
  chopped
extra virgin olive oil, to serve

1 Cook the chopped onion with the olive oil in a covered pan for 8 minutes until softened, stirring occasionally. Add the vegetable stock and petit pois. Bring to the boil, then lower the heat and simmer for 3 minutes.

2 Pour the soup into a blender and whiz until smooth. Return to the pan and reheat gently, stirring in the pesto.

3 To make the tomato bruschetta, toast the ciabatta slices on both sides, then rub with the garlic. Top with the chopped tomatoes and a drizzle of extra virgin olive oil.

4 Pour the soup into warm bowls and top with a little freshly cracked pepper. Serve with the tomato bruschetta.

This is a great soup to make during the short homegrown pea season. At other times, you can, of course, use frozen peas.

Roasted courgette and garlic soup

Serves 4

900g (2lb) courgettes, topped
   and tailed
1 onion, peeled and cut into
   8 wedges
3 garlic cloves (unpeeled)

1 tbsp olive oil
1.2 litres (2 pints) vegetable stock
125g (4oz) frozen petit pois
1 black olive ciabatta
3 tbsp half-fat crème fraîche
freshly ground black pepper

1 Preheat the oven to 200°C (fan oven 180°C), gas mark 6. Thickly slice the courgettes into 2.5cm (1 inch) chunks.

2 Place the courgettes, onion and garlic in a roasting tin and toss with the olive oil. Season with pepper and roast for 30–35 minutes or until golden and tender.

3 Bring the stock to the boil in a saucepan. Add the petit pois, bring back to the boil, then lower the heat and simmer for 2 minutes until tender.

4 Remove the vegetables from the oven, then peel the garlic cloves. Transfer the roasted vegetables and garlic to a food processor or blender, add the stock and petit pois, and blend until smooth. (It may be necessary to purée the soup in batches.) Season with pepper to taste.

5 Cut the ciabatta into rough 2.5cm (1 inch) cubes and place on a baking tray. Toast in the oven for 5 minutes or until crisp. Meanwhile, pour the soup into the saucepan, stir in the crème fraîche and heat gently. Ladle the soup into warm bowls and serve with the croûtons.

Roasting vegetables brings out their natural sweetness and enhances the flavour here. Courgettes are a good source of magnesium, which helps the body absorb other minerals.

Gazpacho with lemon feta bulghar wheat

Serves 4

400g can chopped tomatoes
300ml (½ pint) tomato juice
2 garlic cloves, peeled and crushed
1 tbsp olive oil
2 tbsp white wine vinegar
dash of Tabasco sauce

1 red pepper, halved, deseeded and
  finely diced
100g (3½oz) bulghar wheat
grated zest and juice of ½ lemon
75g (3oz) feta cheese, crumbled
2 tbsp chopped parsley
freshly ground black pepper

1 Place the chopped tomatoes, tomato juice, garlic, olive oil, wine vinegar and Tabasco in a food processor. Process until smooth and season to taste with black pepper. Transfer to a bowl and stir in the red pepper. Cover and chill the soup for 15 minutes or longer.

2 Tip the bulghar wheat into a bowl, pour over 100ml (3½fl oz) boiling water and set aside to soak for 10 minutes. Fork through the bulghar wheat and stir in the lemon zest and juice, feta and parsley. Season with pepper to taste.

3 Ladle the chilled soup into individual bowls. Just before serving, top each portion with a spoonful of lemon and feta bulghar wheat.

This easy Mediterranean chilled soup is ideal for a summer lunch. Bulghar wheat has a crunchy texture and is rich in B vitamins. Feta cheese is a good source of calcium.

Portobello mushroom and bacon soup

Illustrated on previous pages

Serves 4

500g (1lb 2oz) portobello or large field mushrooms, plus 4 whole ones to serve
3 tsp olive oil
1 onion, peeled and finely chopped
1 garlic clove, peeled and crushed
1 litre (1¾ pints) vegetable stock
2 small slices of brown bread, crusts removed
3 tbsp half-fat crème fraîche
4 slices of Parma ham
1 tbsp snipped chives
freshly ground black pepper

1 Peel the portobello mushrooms, set aside the 4 whole ones for serving and slice the rest. Heat 2 tsp of the olive oil in a large pan. Add the onion and garlic, cover and cook for 8 minutes or until soft, stirring occasionally.

2 Stir in the sliced mushrooms and cook for 4 minutes. Add the stock and bring to the boil. Lower the heat and simmer for 10 minutes. Add the bread to the pan and simmer for a further 5 minutes.

3 Pour the soup into a blender and whiz until smooth. Return to the pan, place over a low heat and stir in the crème fraîche. Season well with pepper.

4 Meanwhile, preheat the grill. Place the 4 whole mushrooms, cup-side up, on a baking tray. Drizzle with the remaining olive oil and grind over black pepper. Grill for 3 minutes. Lay the Parma ham on the tray alongside the mushrooms and grill for a further 1 minute or until crispy.

5 Pour the hot soup into warm bowls and top each serving with a grilled mushroom, crispy Parma ham and snipped chives.

This wonderful soup is intensely flavoured with mushrooms and thickened with a little brown bread. Mushrooms are rich in protein and contain B vitamins and useful minerals.

Moorish prawn and chick pea soup

Serves 4

100g (3½oz) cous cous
500g carton passata
400g can chopped tomatoes with
  garlic
2 tsp harissa paste
150ml (¼ pint) white wine
400g can chick peas, drained and
  rinsed

pinch of sugar
grated zest and juice of ½ lemon
2 tbsp extra virgin olive oil
150g (5oz) cooked, peeled prawns
2 tbsp chopped coriander leaves
freshly ground black pepper

1 Put the cous cous into a bowl, pour over 150ml (¼ pint) boiling water and set aside to soak for 5 minutes until the water is absorbed.
2 Meanwhile, pour the passata and chopped tomatoes into a pan and add the harissa paste and wine. Stir in the chick peas and heat gently for 5 minutes. Season to taste with black pepper and a pinch of sugar.
3 Fluff up the cous cous with a fork. Add the lemon zest and juice, olive oil, prawns and coriander and toss to mix. Season with pepper to taste.
4 Pour the spicy tomato soup into four warm bowls, top with the cous cous and serve straightaway.

Inspired by Middle Eastern flavours, this is a great storecupboard recipe that uses canned chick peas and tomatoes.

Garlic mussel bisque

Serves 4
850g (1lb 14oz) fresh mussels
1 tbsp olive oil
3 garlic cloves, peeled and crushed
350g tub fresh arrabiatta sauce
300ml (½ pint) red wine
2 tbsp chopped parsley

1 Discard any mussels with broken shells and those that do not close when
sharply tapped. Scrub the mussels thoroughly in cold water and pull out the
little beards.
2 Heat the olive oil in a large pan, stir in the garlic and cook for 30 seconds.
Add the mussels, arrabiatta sauce and red wine. Cover with a tight-fitting lid
and cook for 2–3 minutes or until the mussels have opened; discard any that
remain closed.
3 Ladle the bisque into serving bowls, scatter over the chopped parsley and
serve straightaway with crusty rustic bread.

This steaming bowl of mussels in a garlic-
infused ready-made sauce is quick to prepare
and tastes delicious. Scatter with chopped
parsley to add freshness.

Smoked fish chowder

Illustrated on previous pages

Serves 4
2 tsp olive oil
1 onion, peeled and finely chopped
500g (1lb 2oz) potatoes, peeled and
    diced
600ml (1 pint) fish stock
300ml (½ pint) semi-skimmed milk
340g can sweetcorn in water,
    drained
450g (1lb) boneless, skinless natural
    smoked haddock or cod, cut into
    bite-sized pieces
2 tbsp chopped parsley
freshly ground black pepper

1 Heat the olive oil in a large pan, add the onion and cook for 5 minutes.
Add the diced potatoes and cook for a further 1 minute. Pour in the stock
and bring to the boil. Lower the heat, cover and simmer for 12–15 minutes
or until the potatoes are tender.
2 With a slotted spoon, remove half the potatoes from the stock and set
aside. Pour the remaining soup into a blender, add the milk and whiz until
smooth. Pour back into the pan.
3 Add the sweetcorn and simmer for 2 minutes. Stir in the fish pieces and
reserved potatoes, and cook for a further 3–4 minutes. Stir in the chopped
parsley and season with pepper to taste. Ladle into warm bowls and serve.

A thick, chunky soup made with naturally smoked haddock or cod, sweetcorn and potato. The fish is full of flavour and protein, yet it's very low in fat. Blitzing half the potatoes with the stock and milk gives the chowder a lovely creamy texture without the addition of cream.

Hot and sour prawn and noodle soup

Serves 4

1 tsp groundnut oil
½ tsp dried red chilli flakes
2.5cm (1 inch) piece fresh root
   ginger, peeled and finely chopped
1 garlic clove, peeled and crushed

1.2 litres (2 pints) chicken stock
250g (9oz) raw tiger prawns, peeled
1 tbsp Thai fish sauce
150g (5oz) sugar snap peas, halved
125g (4oz) rice noodles
grated zest and juice of 1 lime

1 Heat the groundnut oil in a large pan, stir in the dried chilli flakes, chopped ginger and garlic and cook for 1 minute. Add the stock, bring to the boil, then lower the heat and simmer gently for 10 minutes
2 Stir in the raw tiger prawns, fish sauce, sugar snap peas, rice noodles and lime juice and zest. Bring to the boil and simmer for 3 minutes until the prawns are pink and cooked. Serve at once in warm bowls.

Infusing stock with aromatics such as ginger, chilli and garlic creates a speedy oriental style broth. Adding prawns and noodles transforms it into a tempting, flavourful soup.

Curried chicken soup

Serves 4

250g (9oz) skinless chicken breast
   fillets
2 tbsp ready-made curry paste
1 onion, peeled and thinly sliced

1 litre (1¾ pints) chicken stock
175g (6oz) baby leaf spinach
2 tbsp mango chutney
freshly ground black pepper

1 Cut the chicken into thin strips and set aside. Heat the curry paste in a pan, stir in the onion, then cover and cook for 5 minutes, stirring occasionally. Add the chicken strips and cook, stirring, for 1 minute.

2 Pour in the stock and bring to the boil. Lower the heat and simmer for about 5 minutes.

3 Stir in the spinach and mango chutney. Heat through until the spinach has just wilted and season with pepper to taste. Ladle into warm bowls and serve with warm chapattis.

Buy good quality stock products, especially salt-free or low-salt stocks. Ready-made fresh stocks are available from supermarkets.

Chicken noodle and pak choi soup

Serves 4

1.2 litres (2 pints) miso broth
1 tbsp grated fresh root ginger
2 tbsp good quality soy sauce
250g (9oz) boneless, skinless chicken
  breast, cut into thin strips
125g (4oz) Thai stir-fry rice noodles
200g (7oz) pak choi, divided into
  leaves
½ bunch of spring onions, chopped
2 tsp sesame oil
freshly ground black pepper

1 Make up the miso broth according to the packet instructions. Pour into a large pan and add the ginger, soy sauce and chicken strips. Bring to the boil and simmer for 3 minutes.

2 Add the rice noodles and cook for 1 minute. Add the pak choi and cook for a further 1 minute. Stir in the spring onions and simmer for a final minute. Stir in the sesame oil, season with pepper to taste and serve in warm bowls.

Rice noodles and chicken soak up the flavours in this simple broth. Miso is a Japanese food that is made from fermented soya beans. It is widely available in sachet form; for this stock base, use two or more sachets to taste.

healthy
fish

Lemon and bay scented hoki

Serves 4

4 skinless hoki or haddock fillets,
  each about 150g (5oz)
8 bay leaves
1 unwaxed lemon, thinly sliced
4 tbsp dry vermouth
freshly ground black pepper

For the mash

900g (2lb) potatoes, peeled
4 tbsp natural yogurt
3 tbsp warm milk
2 tbsp wholegrain mustard

1 For the mash, cut the potatoes into even-sized chunks and place in a pan of cold water. Bring to the boil, lower the heat and simmer for 20 minutes or until tender. Preheat the oven to 190°C (fan oven 170°C), gas mark 5.

2 Meanwhile, arrange the hoki or haddock fillets in an ovenproof dish and season with black pepper. Place 2 bay leaves on each fish fillet and cover with slices of lemon. Drizzle over the vermouth and cover with damp greaseproof paper. Bake for 10–12 minutes or until the fish is just opaque.

3 Drain the potatoes well and tip back into the pan. Mash over a gentle heat until smooth. Stir in the yogurt, milk and mustard, then season to taste.

4 Serve the hoki with the flavoured mash, and sugar snaps or mangetout.

Hoki is a firm white fish from New Zealand, similar to cod and well suited to baking. A healthy way to make creamy and tasty mash, without adding lashings of butter and cream, is to stir in mustard and natural yogurt.

Mustard crusted cod with roasted peppers

Illustrated on previous pages

Serves 4
75g (3oz) cous cous
3 red peppers
1 tbsp olive oil
2 tbsp Dijon mustard
4 cod steaks, each about 150g (5oz)
350g (12oz) runner beans, trimmed
   and sliced
squeeze of lemon juice
freshly ground black pepper

1 Preheat the oven to 200°C (fan oven 180°C), gas mark 6. Place the cous cous in a small bowl, pour over 100ml (3½fl oz) cold water and leave to soak for 5 minutes.
2 Halve, core and deseed the peppers, then cut each half into 4 strips. Place the red peppers in a roasting tray, drizzle over the olive oil and toss well to coat in the oil. Roast for 25–30 minutes.
3 Spread the mustard evenly over the cod steaks, sprinkle the cous cous on top and press to adhere. Set to one side.
4 Toss the green beans in with the peppers and season with black pepper. Sit the cod steaks on top, cous cous side up, and squeeze over the lemon juice. Roast for 8–10 minutes.
5 Meanwhile, preheat the grill. Flash the roasting tray under the grill for 1–2 minutes or until the cous cous crust is golden. Serve immediately.

Cod steaks keep deliciously moist underneath an unusual crisp topping of cous cous, which is pre-soaked in cold rather than hot water for extra crunch. Red peppers and runner beans provide colour and plenty of vitamin C.

Parma roasted cod with bean and rocket salad

Serves 4

4 boneless, skinless cod loins, each
   about 150g (5oz)
12 sage leaves
4 slices of Parma ham
2 x 300g cans flageolet beans,
   drained and rinsed

2 garlic cloves, peeled and crushed
2 tbsp extra virgin olive oil
1 tbsp lemon juice
125g (4oz) rocket leaves
freshly ground black pepper

1 Preheat the oven to 220°C (fan oven 200°C), gas mark 7. Season the cod
with black pepper. Arrange 3 sage leaves on each cod fillet and wrap in a
slice of Parma ham. Place in a roasting tin and roast for 6–8 minutes,
depending on the thickness of the cod.

2 In the meantime, tip the flageolet beans into a pan. Add the garlic and stir
over a medium heat for 2 minutes or until heated through. Add the olive oil
and lemon juice and season well. Add the rocket and stir through the beans.

3 Divide the bean and rocket salad between four serving plates and place a
portion of roasted Parma-wrapped cod alongside. Serve straightaway.

Parma ham and meaty fish complement each
other very well. Garlic and lemon enhance the
flavour of the flageolet beans, and fresh rocket
provides a delicious, peppery contrast.

Smoked haddock tortilla

Serves 4–6

450g (1lb) medium waxy potatoes, peeled and halved
225g (8oz) skinless, naturally smoked haddock fillet
2 tsp olive oil
2 Spanish onions, peeled and finely sliced
6 eggs
freshly ground black pepper

For the salsa

300g (11oz) baby broad beans, cooked and skinned
3 plum tomatoes, chopped
1 tbsp tomato ketchup
good dash of Tabasco sauce

1 Par-boil the potatoes in water for about 8–10 minutes until only just tender, then drain. When cool enough to handle, thickly slice the potatoes. Cut the smoked haddock into thin slivers and set aside.
2 Heat the olive oil in a large non-stick frying pan (suitable for use under the grill). Add the onions, cover and steam-fry for 5 minutes, stirring occasionally. Remove the lid and cook for 8 minutes or until the onions are soft and golden. Stir in the sliced potatoes and cook for a further 2 minutes.
3 Preheat the grill. Beat the eggs in a bowl and season with pepper. Pour the beaten eggs into the frying pan and scatter the smoked haddock slivers on top. Cook the tortilla, gently shaking the pan, for 4 minutes or until it is just set underneath.
4 Place the pan under the grill and cook the tortilla for a further 3 minutes or until golden and just set on top. Meanwhile, mix the salsa ingredients together in a bowl and season with pepper to taste.
5 Turn out the tortilla on to a warm serving plate and cut into wedges. Serve immediately, with the tomato and broad bean salsa.

Lemon and sardine chunky fish pittas

Serves 4

100g (3½oz) cream cheese
finely grated zest of 1 lemon
2 x 120g cans sardines in tomato
  sauce

4 wholemeal pitta breads
olive oil, to brush
100g (3½oz) rocket leaves
freshly ground black pepper
lemon wedges, to serve

1 In a bowl, mix the cream cheese with the lemon zest and pepper to taste.
Gently stir in the canned sardines, keeping the mixture chunky.
2 Brush the pitta breads with a little olive oil and cook on a hot non-stick
griddle pan for 1 minute on each side until charred and crispy.
3 Split the pitta breads and divide the sardine mixture and rocket leaves
between them. Serve at once, with lemon wedges.

With a little imagination, a nutritious can of
sardines can be transformed into a speedy
supper. Rocket leaves add a peppery freshness.

Baked oaty mackerel fillets with apple sauce

Serves 4
8 mackerel fillets
4 tbsp wholegrain mustard
10 oat cakes, crushed

For the apple sauce
4 large Cox's apples
grated zest and juice of ½ lemon
2 tsp thyme leaves
freshly ground black pepper

1 Preheat the oven to 200°C (fan oven 180°C), gas mark 6. Lay the mackerel fillets, flesh-side up, on a non-stick baking sheet. Spread with the mustard and coat with the crushed oat cakes. Bake for 10 minutes.
2 Meanwhile, peel, core and chop the apples and cook in a non-stick pan with the lemon zest and juice for 5–6 minutes until tender but holding their shape. Stir in the thyme leaves and pepper to taste.
3 Serve the mackerel with the apple sauce and green beans or mangetout.

Like other fresh oily fish, mackerel is rich in beneficial omega-3 oils. It is also widely available and relatively inexpensive. Buy fresh mackerel on the day you intend to eat it.

Griddled mackerel with spinach lentils

Serves 4

2 tbsp coriander seeds

1 tbsp coarsely ground black pepper

4 tbsp roughly chopped flat leaf
parsley

8 small mackerel fillets

1 tbsp olive oil

For the spinach lentils

1 tbsp sunflower oil

1 large onion, peeled and chopped

4 garlic cloves, peeled and crushed

1 tbsp garam masala

350g (12oz) split red lentils, rinsed

1.2 litres (2 pints) vegetable stock

225g (8oz) spinach leaves, roughly
chopped

1 To release the flavour from the coriander seeds, pound with a pestle and mortar, or place them in a strong plastic bag and crush with a rolling pin. Tip into a bowl and mix with the pepper and parsley.

2 Rub the flesh side of the mackerel fillets with the olive oil, then sprinkle with the spice mix and press to adhere. Set to one side.

3 For the spinach lentils, heat the sunflower oil in a large pan. Add the onion and steam-fry for 5 minutes. Add the garlic and garam masala and cook for a further 1 minute. Stir in the lentils and stock, bring to the boil and simmer for 15–20 minutes or until the lentils are just tender.

4 Heat a non-stick griddle pan over a medium heat. When hot, add the mackerel fillets, skin-side down, and cook for 2–3 minutes. Turn carefully and cook for a further 2 minutes.

5 Stir the spinach into the lentils and cook briefly until just wilted. Spoon on to four serving plates and top each serving with two mackerel fillets.

Lentils are extremely nutritious, being a good source of protein, fibre, vitamin B, calcium, iron and phosphorus.

Salmon sushi

Serves 4

400g (14oz) skinless salmon fillet
2 tbsp extra virgin olive oil
juice of 1 lemon
juice of 1 lime
4 spring onions, trimmed and finely
  sliced

1 red chilli, deseeded and diced
225g (8oz) Thai fragrant rice
1 ripe avocado, halved, stoned,
  peeled and thinly sliced
freshly ground black pepper
coriander sprigs, to serve

1 Thinly slice the salmon fillet against the grain and lay in a shallow dish.
Mix the olive oil with the lemon juice, half the lime juice, the spring onions,
red chilli and some pepper. Spoon over the salmon, cover and leave to
marinate in a cool place for 20 minutes.
2 Meanwhile, cook the Thai rice according to the packet instructions. Allow
to cool slightly, then toss with the rest of the lime juice and some pepper.
Pack the rice firmly into cups, then unmould on to individual plates.
3 Surround the rice with the marinated salmon and avocado slices, spooning
the marinade over. Garnish with coriander sprigs to serve.

Very fresh salmon is essential for this
appealing dish. It makes an attractive starter
or light, summer lunch.

Roasted salmon on black toasts

Serves 4

575g (1¼lb) thick salmon fillet
juice of ½ lemon
1 tbsp olive oil
4 thick slices of ciabatta bread
4 tbsp black olive tapenade
freshly ground black pepper

For the salad

75g (3oz) watercress, trimmed
1 red onion, peeled and thinly sliced
2 large oranges, segmented

1 Preheat the oven to 200°C (fan oven 180°C), gas mark 6. Cut the salmon into 8 strips and lay these on a non-stick baking tray. Drizzle over the lemon juice and half the olive oil, and season with pepper. Bake for 8–10 minutes or until the salmon is just cooked.

2 For the salad, toss the watercress sprigs, onion slices and orange segments together in a bowl. Season with a little pepper.

3 Meanwhile, heat a large non-stick griddle pan and brush with the remaining olive oil. Griddle the ciabatta slices for 2 minutes on each side or until golden and crisp. Spread the ciabatta toasts with the olive tapenade and place on four serving plates. Lay two strips of salmon on each toast. Top with the watercress salad and serve.

Steam, griddle or oven bake, rather than deep-fry fish, for a healthy lunch or supper. Here baked salmon strips are served on tangy olive tapenade toasts.

Pan-fried smoked salmon with avocado

Serves 4

2 plum tomatoes
3 tbsp olive oil
bunch of chives, roughly chopped
juice of ½ lemon

225g (8oz) smoked salmon slices
120g bag of mixed salad leaves
1 large, ripe avocado, halved, stoned,
  peeled and sliced
freshly ground black pepper

1 Immerse the tomatoes in a bowl of boiling hot water for 30 seconds or so, remove and peel away the skin. Halve, deseed and thinly slice the tomatoes.
2 Heat 2½ tbsp olive oil in a small pan. Add the plum tomatoes, chives and a good squeeze of lemon juice. Season to taste and gently heat through.
3 Heat the remaining olive oil in a non-stick frying pan. Add the salmon pieces, grind over a little black pepper and cook for 30 seconds on each side.
4 Divide the salad leaves between four serving plates and top with the avocado slices. Arrange the smoked salmon slices, slightly folded, on the avocado. Spoon over the hot tomato and chive dressing and serve at once.

This is smoked salmon with a difference – flashed in a hot pan, then served with an avocado salad. Avocado is rich in vitamin E, high in beneficial monounsaturated fatty acids and a good source of potassium.

Chilli salmon with courgette pilaf

Serves 4

225g (8oz) basmati rice
2 tsp olive oil
1 onion, peeled and finely chopped
2 garlic cloves,.peeled and crushed
4 courgettes, chopped
1 small unwaxed lemon, cut into
  quarters

600ml (1 pint) vegetable stock
4 skinless salmon fillets, each about
  150g (5oz)
4 tsp sweet chilli dipping sauce
3 tbsp chopped coriander leaves
freshly ground black pepper

1 Rinse the rice in a sieve under cold running water and set aside to drain.
2 Heat the olive oil in a large shallow pan. Add the onion and garlic and
cook gently for 5 minutes or until softened. Stir in the rice, courgettes and
lemon quarters, and cook for 1 minute.
3 Pour in the stock and bring to the boil. Cover and cook over a low heat for
15 minutes until all the stock has been absorbed and the rice is tender.
4 Meanwhile, preheat the grill. Lay the salmon on a non-stick baking sheet,
grind over black pepper and spread each fillet with 1 tsp of chilli sauce. Grill
for 5–6 minutes or until cooked through and lightly charred.
5 Season the pilaf to taste and stir in the chopped coriander. Spoon on to
four serving plates, discarding the lemon if you prefer, and place the salmon
fillets alongside.

Just a touch of chilli really brings out all the
fresh flavours in this dish, which is packed
with protein and vitamins.

Seared trout with sweet potato wedges

Serves 4

3 medium sweet potatoes, scrubbed
2 tbsp Worcestershire sauce
3 tbsp olive oil
2 large rainbow trout, filleted
juice of 1 large orange
juice of ½ lemon
2 tbsp small capers, drained
1 tbsp chopped parsley
freshly ground black pepper

1 Preheat the oven to 200°C (fan oven 180°C), gas mark 6. Cut the sweet potatoes into thick wedges and place in a large bowl. Add the Worcestershire sauce and 2 tbsp olive oil and toss to mix. Transfer to a large roasting tray and season with pepper. Bake for 30–35 minutes until golden and crisp.
2 Meanwhile, heat a non-stick griddle pan until very hot. Brush the flesh side of the trout fillets with the remaining olive oil and season well with pepper. Place the fillets, flesh-side down, in the pan and cook for 2 minutes on each side. Remove from the pan and arrange on serving plates.
3 Add the orange and lemon juices, capers and parsley to the pan and allow to bubble for a few seconds. Spoon the warm dressing over the trout fillets and serve, with the roasted sweet potato wedges.

Trout is another oily fish that is high in protein and contains those helpful omega-3 oils. You can use regular potatoes rather than sweet potatoes if you prefer – they'll just take a little longer to cook.

Anchovy and tuna jackets

Serves 4

4 baking potatoes, scrubbed
1 tsp olive oil
2 x 160g cans yellow fin tuna in
  spring water, drained
400g can cannellini beans, drained
  and rinsed

50g can anchovy fillets, drained
  (reserving oil) and finely chopped
1 red onion, peeled and finely sliced
grated zest and juice of 1 lemon
4 tbsp chopped parsley
freshly ground black pepper

1 Preheat the oven to 200°C (fan oven 180°C), gas mark 6. Rub the baking potatoes all over with the olive oil and bake for about 1 hour until tender.
2 Meanwhile, flake the tuna and toss with the cannellini beans, chopped anchovies and their oil, red onion, lemon zest and juice, chopped parsley and pepper to taste.
3 Split the baked potatoes, fill with the tuna salad and serve straightaway.

Canned oily fish is a great convenience food. Here baked potatoes are filled with a tuna salad for a healthy, sustaining supper.

Seared tuna with green beans and basil

Serves 4

1 tsp olive oil

4 fresh tuna steaks, each about 150g (5oz)

2 tbsp balsamic vinegar

450g (1lb) baby new potatoes

225g (8oz) French beans, trimmed

200g (7oz) cherry tomatoes, halved

½ bunch of spring onions, trimmed and finely chopped

freshly ground black pepper

For the pistou

2 garlic cloves, peeled

large bunch of basil

2 tbsp extra virgin olive oil

juice of ½ orange

1 Sprinkle the olive oil over the tuna steaks and rub in with your fingertips. Place in a non-metallic dish, grind over pepper and drizzle over the balsamic vinegar. Set aside for 15 minutes.

2 Boil the potatoes until tender, then drain and set aside to cool. Add the French beans to a pan of boiling water and blanch for 2–3 minutes, then drain and refresh in cold water. Drain thoroughly and tip into a bowl. Add the potatoes, tomatoes and spring onions, and toss to mix.

3 To make the pistou, put the garlic, basil, olive oil and orange juice into a small food processor and process until blended. Season to taste.

4 Heat a non-stick griddle pan until it is really hot. Add the tuna steaks and sear for about 2 minutes on each side until cooked.

5 Pour two-thirds of the pistou over the salad and gently mix together. Arrange the salad on four serving plates, top each with a seared tuna steak and spoon over the remaining pistou. Serve at once.

Fresh tuna is rich in valuable omega-3 fish oils. These oils are beneficial because they help to maintain a healthy heart.

Prawn red Thai noodles

Illustrated on previous pages

Serves 4

1½ tbsp Thai red curry paste
4 tbsp passata
125g (4oz) Thai rice noodles
225g (8oz) raw tiger prawns, peeled and deveined
200g (7oz) sugar snap peas, halved lengthways
150g (5oz) bean sprouts
50g (2oz) cashew nuts, toasted
lime wedges, to serve

1 Mix the Thai red curry paste and passata together in a small bowl and set aside. Cook the rice noodles according to the packet instructions and drain.
2 Meanwhile, heat a non-stick wok until very hot, then add the peeled tiger prawns and cook for 1 minute. Add half of the red Thai paste mix and stir-fry for a further 1 minute. Add the sugar snap peas with 2 tbsp water and stir-fry for 2 minutes.
3 Stir in the rice noodles, bean sprouts, cashew nuts and remaining red Thai paste mix. Toss over a high heat for a further 2 minutes until piping hot. Divide the prawn noodles between four warm bowls and serve immediately, with lime wedges.

Rice noodles are combined with juicy tiger prawns and crunchy vegetables for a tempting stir-fry that can be made in minutes.

Teriyaki swordfish with spinach

Serves 4

4 swordfish steaks, each about
  150g (5oz)
2 tsp olive oil
4 tbsp teriyaki sauce
1 garlic clove, peeled and crushed

2 tbsp Madras curry paste
1 tbsp tomato purée
400ml can reduced-fat coconut milk
squeeze of lemon juice
350g (12oz) baby leaf spinach
freshly ground black pepper

1 Place the swordfish steaks in a non-metallic dish and season with pepper. Mix together the olive oil, teriyaki sauce and garlic, then drizzle over the swordfish. Set aside for 5 minutes.

2 Heat a medium saucepan, add the curry paste and tomato purée and fry for 30 seconds. Pour in the coconut milk and simmer for 5 minutes. Finish with a squeeze of lemon juice to taste.

3 Heat a non-stick griddle pan until very hot. Add the swordfish steaks and griddle for 2–3 minutes on each side. Pour in the teriyaki marinade and allow to bubble, spooning it over the swordfish steaks to glaze.

4 In the meantime, put the spinach in a large pan (with just the water clinging to the leaves after washing), cover and cook for 30 seconds or until just wilted. Stir and season with a little pepper.

5 Place the wilted spinach in the centre of each serving plate, top with the swordfish steaks and drizzle over the coconut gravy.

This is a real infusion of flavours. A teriyaki marinade adds an oriental flavour to meaty swordfish, while the accompanying coconut gravy is fragrant with aromatic spices.

healthy
chicken
and
turkey

Citrus roasted chicken with tzatziki

Serves 4

1 free-range or organic chicken,
    about 1.6kg (3½lb)
handful of thyme sprigs
1 large orange, cut into quarters
2 unwaxed lemons, halved
freshly ground black pepper

For the tzatziki

½ cucumber
200g (7oz) Greek yogurt
1 garlic clove, peeled and crushed
1 tbsp extra virgin olive oil
20g (¾oz) mint leaves, chopped
lemon juice, to taste

1 Preheat the oven to 200°C (fan oven 180°C), gas mark 6. Lay the chicken, breast-side down, on a board. Using poultry shears or a sharp pair of scissors, cut down either side of the backbone. Turn the chicken over and press to flatten, using the heel of your hand. Season generously with pepper and place, breast-side down, in a roasting tin or tray. Scatter the thyme over and roast for 30 minutes.

2 Remove the roasting tin from the oven and reduce the setting to 180°C (fan oven 160°C), gas mark 4. Squeeze the juice from the orange and lemons over the chicken, then add the spent citrus peel pieces to the tin and turn the chicken over. Roast for a further 30–40 minutes until the chicken is cooked through. To test, pierce the thickest part of the thigh with a skewer: the juices that exude should run clear; if they are at all pink, return to the oven for a little longer.

3 Meanwhile, make the tzatziki. Coarsely grate the cucumber, squeeze out the excess liquid, then place in a bowl. Add the yogurt, garlic, olive oil, mint and lemon juice, and black pepper to taste.

4 Remove the chicken from the oven, cover with foil and leave to rest in a warm place for 10 minutes before serving. Serve the chicken with the tzatziki, and a watercress salad if you like.

Removing the backbone from the chicken and flattening the bird helps it to cook more evenly and quickly, keeping the breast meat moist.

Apple roast chicken and new potatoes

Illustrated on previous pages

Serves 4

4 free-range or organic chicken
  thighs
4 free-range or organic chicken
  drumsticks
juice of ½ lemon
1 tbsp olive oil
2 red onions, peeled, halved and each
  half cut into 4 chunks

200ml (7fl oz) dry cider
150ml (¼ pint) chicken stock
3 medium Cox's apples, cored and
  cut into 6 wedges
3 rosemary sprigs

For the roasted new potatoes
675g (1½lb) Charlotte potatoes,
  halved lengthways
2 tsp olive oil

1 Preheat the oven to 200°C (fan oven 180°C), gas mark 6. For the roasted
potatoes, place the potatoes in a roasting tray and drizzle with the 2 tsp olive
oil. Roast in the top of the oven for 35–40 minutes until tender and crisp.
2 Place the chicken on a rack over a roasting tin and squeeze over the lemon
juice. Roast, skin-side up, on a shelf below the potatoes for 20–25 minutes.
3 Meanwhile, heat the olive oil in a pan and steam-fry the onions over a
medium heat for 10–15 minutes until beginning to soften and brown.
Uncover and pour in the cider and stock. Bring to the boil and simmer
gently for 5 minutes.
4 Transfer the chicken to a plate. Remove any fat from the roasting tin, then
add the onion and cider mixture. Add the apples and rosemary, then sit the
chicken pieces, skin-side up, on top. Roast for a further 15–20 minutes until
the chicken is cooked through. Serve with the roasted potatoes.

The chicken pieces are first roasted on a rack
to crisp the skin and lose as much fat as
possible, then on a bed of apples flavoured
with rosemary and cider.

Maple roasted poussins with garlic

Serves 4

4 poussins

4 rosemary sprigs

4 garlic cloves, peeled and lightly
 crushed

2 tbsp maple syrup

1 tbsp Dijon mustard

2 tsp olive oil

freshly ground black pepper

1 Preheat the oven to 200°C (fan oven 180°C), gas mark 6. Stuff the poussin cavities with the rosemary and garlic, then loosely tie up the legs with kitchen string.

2 In a small bowl, mix together the maple syrup, mustard, olive oil and some black pepper. Place the poussins in a roasting tray and pour over the maple syrup glaze.

3 Roast in the oven for 40–45 minutes, basting occasionally, until golden and cooked through. Serve with new potatoes and a salad or green vegetable.

Poussins make a change from chicken. Here they are flavoured simply with rosemary and garlic, and glazed with maple syrup – to delicious effect.

Sun-blushed chicken pockets

Serves 4

4 skinless chicken breast fillets, each
  about 150g (5oz)
4 tbsp low-fat cream cheese
12 sun-blushed tomatoes, roughly
  chopped
4 slices of pancetta
freshly ground black pepper

For the greens

1 tbsp olive oil
2 garlic cloves, peeled and crushed
300g (11oz) cavolo nero, spring
  greens or green cabbage, cored
  and finely shredded
squeeze of lemon juice

1 Preheat the oven to 200°C (fan oven 180°C), gas mark 6. Remove the small fillet from the underside of each chicken breast and set aside. Make a vertical cut down the length of each chicken breast, but not all the way through, to form a pocket.

2 Mix the cream cheese with the tomatoes and season with pepper. Put a spoonful into each chicken breast pocket. Fold over the flaps of the pocket and cover with the reserved fillets to enclose the filling.

3 Loosely wrap a slice of pancetta around each chicken breast. Heat a large non-stick frying pan (preferably ovenproof), add the chicken and sear for 2 minutes on each side until golden. Transfer to the oven and bake for 12–15 minutes or until the chicken is cooked through. (If your pan isn't ovenproof, transfer the chicken to a roasting tray.)

4 Just before serving, heat the olive oil in a non-stick wok, add the garlic and fry gently for 30 seconds. Add the shredded cabbage and stir-fry for 3–4 minutes until wilted, but still retaining a bite. Add a squeeze of lemon juice and pepper to taste. Serve the chicken parcels on the stir-fried cabbage.

Chicken breasts are filled with sun-blushed tomatoes and low-fat cream cheese, then wrapped in pancetta and baked. A healthy stir-fry of Italian greens is the ideal complement.

Tapenade chicken with lemon Puy lentils

Serves 4

4 skinless chicken breast fillets,
  each about 150g (5oz)
4 tbsp black olive tapenade
4 slices of Parma ham
4 bay leaves
1 tsp olive oil
freshly ground black pepper

For the lemon Puy lentils

300g (11oz) Puy lentils
1 litre (1¾ pints) chicken or
  vegetable stock
4 tbsp extra virgin olive oil
grated zest and juice of 1 lemon
225g (8oz) baby or young leaf
  spinach

1 Preheat the oven to 200°C (fan oven 180°C), gas mark 6. For the lemon Puy lentils, put the lentils in a pan with the stock. Bring to the boil and simmer for 20–25 minutes until the lentils are tender.

2 Meanwhile, place the chicken breasts on a board and remove the small fillet from the underside of each breast; set aside. Make a vertical cut down the length of the chicken breast, but not all the way through, to create a pocket. Season all over with pepper.

3 Place 1 tbsp of olive tapenade in the pocket of each chicken breast. Fold over the flaps of the pocket and cover with the reserved fillets to enclose the filling. Wrap a piece of Parma ham around each chicken breast and tuck in a bay leaf. Brush lightly with the olive oil.

4 Heat a large non-stick frying pan (preferably ovenproof), add the chicken and sear for 2 minutes on each side until golden. Transfer to the oven and bake for 12–15 minutes or until the chicken is cooked through. (If your pan isn't ovenproof, transfer the chicken to a roasting tray.)

5 When cooked, drain the lentils and return to the pan. Stir in the extra virgin olive oil, lemon zest and juice. Return to the heat and gently warm through, then add the spinach and stir until wilted. Season with pepper to taste. Serve the chicken with the Puy lentils.

Tapenade, or black olive paste, makes a tasty stuffing for chicken.

Chicken and prune ragout

Serves 4

3 large red onions, peeled and each
   cut into 8 wedges
2 tbsp olive oil
8 whole garlic cloves (unpeeled)
4 skinless chicken breast fillets,
   each about 150g (5oz)

200ml (7fl oz) red wine
250g (9oz) ready-to-eat prunes
4 thyme sprigs
150ml (¼ pint) hot chicken stock

1 Preheat the oven to 200°C (fan oven 180°C), gas mark 6. Put the onion wedges in a roasting tin and drizzle 1 tbsp olive oil over them. Roast for 20 minutes, then add the garlic cloves and roast for a further 10 minutes.
2 Meanwhile, using a small knife, slash the top of each chicken breast in a criss-cross fashion, taking care not to cut all the way through. Put the chicken in a shallow dish and pour over the remaining olive oil and 50ml (2fl oz) of the red wine. Leave to marinate for 20 minutes.
3 Heat a large non-stick frying pan over a medium-high heat. Remove the chicken from the marinade, add to the frying pan and sear for 2 minutes on each side or until golden brown.
4 Scatter the prunes and thyme over the roasted onions and garlic, then pour over the remaining wine and the stock. Place the seared chicken breasts on top and bake in the oven for 15–20 minutes or until the chicken is cooked through. Serve with cous cous, rice or fluffy mashed potato.

I am a huge fan of ready-to-eat juicy prunes. They are rich in fibre and antioxidants, and go well in savoury dishes. Don't be put off by the number of garlic cloves here – they mellow and sweeten as they roast in their skins.

Polenta crusted chicken

Serves 4

8 skinless chicken thigh fillets
juice of 1 lime
2 tbsp Cajun spice
4 tbsp polenta
½ tbsp olive oil
1 large onion, peeled and sliced
3 red peppers, cored, deseeded and
  sliced

pinch of sugar
1 large garlic clove, peeled and
  crushed
150ml (¼ pint) vegetable stock
150ml (¼ pint) tomato juice
freshly ground black pepper
watercress sprigs, to serve

1 Preheat the oven to 200°C (fan oven 180°C), gas mark 6. Open out the chicken thighs and squeeze the lime juice over. Sprinkle with half of the Cajun spice and re-roll.

2 Toss the polenta with the remaining Cajun spice and spread out on a plate. Turn the rolled chicken thighs in the polenta to coat evenly, pressing with your fingertips to ensure the coating adheres. Transfer the chicken to a roasting tin and bake for 35–40 minutes until golden and cooked through.

3 Meanwhile, heat the olive oil in a large pan. Add the onion and red peppers, cover with a damp piece of greaseproof paper and put the lid on the pan. Cook gently for 15 minutes until very soft. Stir in the sugar, garlic, stock and tomato juice. Cover again and cook for a further 10 minutes. Cool slightly, then whiz in a blender or food processor until smooth. Season with pepper to taste.

4 Serve the polenta crusted chicken with the red pepper gravy and watercress. Roasted new potatoes (see page 128) are a good accompaniment.

These crispy baked chicken thighs, coated in spiced polenta, are delicious. Polenta is free from gluten – especially useful for anyone with an intolerance to this wheat-based protein.

Steamed tarragon chicken breasts

Serves 4

4 skinless chicken breast fillets,
   each about 150g (5oz)
4 leeks, trimmed
1 tbsp olive oil
150ml (¼ pint) white wine
8 tarragon sprigs
freshly ground black pepper

For the sauce

5 tbsp half-fat crème fraîche
1 garlic clove, peeled and crushed
2 tsp Dijon mustard
2 tbsp chopped tarragon

1 Cut each of the chicken breasts lengthways into 4 pieces. Slice the leeks into 2cm (¾ inch) pieces. Heat the olive oil in a large sauté pan, add the leeks and gently steam-fry for 10 minutes. Add the wine and boil rapidly until it has almost totally reduced.

2 Scatter the tarragon sprigs over the leeks and lay the chicken pieces on top. Season with black pepper. Cover with a damp piece of greaseproof paper and put the lid on the pan. Cook very gently for 15–18 minutes until the chicken is cooked.

3 Meanwhile, to make the sauce, combine the crème fraîche, garlic, mustard and chopped tarragon in a bowl and stir until evenly blended. Season with pepper to taste.

4 Serve the steamed chicken and leeks with a generous spoonful of the creamy tarragon sauce, and baked potatoes.

Gently steaming chicken breasts with leeks and aromatic tarragon in one pot is a healthy way of cooking and keeps the meat moist and full of taste. A creamy, low-fat mustard and tarragon sauce is the perfect partner.

Chicken korma

Serves 4

2 tbsp sunflower oil

2 large onions, peeled and finely sliced

12 skinless chicken thigh fillets

3 garlic cloves, peeled and crushed

1 tbsp garam masala

2 tsp ground turmeric

1 bay leaf

450ml (¾ pint) chicken stock

75ml (2½fl oz) natural yogurt

150ml (¼ pint) reduced-fat coconut milk

2 tbsp ground almonds

20g (¾oz) mint leaves, chopped

For the relish

4 ripe tomatoes, chopped

1 small red onion, peeled and finely chopped

20g (¾oz) coriander leaves, torn

squeeze of lemon juice

freshly ground black pepper

1 Heat 1 tbsp oil in a large, shallow pan. Add the onions and steam-fry for 10 minutes until softened. Uncover and fry for a further 5 minutes until beginning to brown.

2 Meanwhile, halve the chicken thigh fillets. Heat the remaining sunflower oil in a large non-stick frying pan, add the chicken pieces and sauté for about 2 minutes on each side or until golden.

3 Add the garlic and spices to the onions and fry, stirring, for 1 minute, then add the sautéed chicken and bay leaf. Pour in the stock and bring to the boil. Simmer gently for 15–20 minutes or until the chicken is cooked.

4 In the meantime, prepare the relish. Combine the tomatoes, red onion and coriander in a bowl. Toss to mix and add lemon juice and black pepper to taste. Set aside.

5 Stir the yogurt, coconut milk, almonds and mint into the korma. Warm through, but do not boil or the coconut milk will separate. Season to taste and serve straightaway, with the relish and basmati rice or chapattis.

This creamy korma is much lower in fat than you would think because it is enriched with half-fat coconut milk, natural yogurt and almonds. If you want more heat, add chilli flakes with the spices.

Chicken and sesame stir-fry with noodles

Serves 4

2 large skinless chicken breast fillets
1 tbsp olive oil
1 garlic clove, peeled and crushed
5cm (2 inch) piece fresh root ginger,
   peeled and finely chopped
225g (8oz) broccoli florets
2 large carrots

1 bunch of spring onions, trimmed
250g (9oz) medium egg noodles
2 tbsp soy sauce
1 tbsp thin honey
juice of 1 orange
1 tbsp sesame seeds, toasted
freshly ground black pepper

1 Cut the chicken breasts into thin strips and place in a bowl with the olive oil, garlic and ginger. Toss to mix and set to one side.

2 Put the broccoli florets in a heatproof bowl, cover with boiling water and leave to stand for 1 minute. Drain, refresh under cold running water and drain well. Cut the carrots into thin matchstick strips. Halve the spring onions and cut into strips lengthways.

3 Heat a large non-stick wok or non-stick sauté pan, add the chicken and stir-fry for 2 minutes. Add the carrots, broccoli and 1 tbsp water. Cover with a lid and steam-fry for 4–5 minutes until the chicken is cooked, adding the spring onions for the last minute.

4 Meanwhile, cook the noodles according to the packet instructions. In a bowl, mix together the soy sauce, honey and orange juice.

5 Drain the noodles thoroughly and add to the pan with the soy mixture. Toss well until everything is piping hot. Season and scatter over the sesame seeds. Serve at once, in warm bowls.

This stir-fry is fast, colourful and packed with nutrients. Broccoli is an excellent source of vitamins – including antioxidants – and minerals. Stir-frying helps to preserve the vitamin C content.

Chicken and avocado on rye

Serves 4

4 slices of rye bread

225g (8oz) cooked chicken or turkey
  breast, sliced

For the guacamole

1 large, ripe avocado, halved, stoned,
  peeled and chopped

4 cherry tomatoes, quartered

squeeze of lime juice

1 shallot, peeled and finely chopped

1 small garlic clove, peeled and
  crushed

dash of Tabasco sauce

2 tbsp Greek yogurt

freshly ground black pepper

To serve

tomato chutney (optional)

lime wedges, to serve

1 Place a slice of rye bread on each plate and top with the cooked, sliced chicken or turkey.

2 To make the guacamole, toss the avocado and tomatoes with the lime juice, shallot, garlic, Tabasco, yogurt and pepper to taste.

3 Spoon the guacamole on top of the chicken and add a spoonful of tomato chutney if you like. Accompany with lime wedges.

Top rye bread with cooked chicken, homemade guacamole and tomato chutney to make a satisfying, nutritious lunch.

Chicken and artichoke pain bagnes

Serves 4

4 wholemeal baps
1 garlic clove, peeled and halved
225g (8oz) cooked chicken breast,
  thinly sliced
3 plum tomatoes, thinly sliced
4 roasted artichokes in oil, drained
  and quartered
few basil leaves, torn
freshly ground black pepper

1 Cut each bap horizontally into 3 slices and toast the slices on both sides, then rub with the cut garlic clove.

2 Layer half the chicken, tomatoes and artichokes on the bap bases. Season with pepper and scatter with torn basil. Press on the middle toasted bap slices and repeat the filling layer.

3 Position the bap tops, press down gently and serve.

Toasted wholemeal baps are filled with cooked chicken, artichokes and plum tomatoes for a healthy, speedy lunch.

Spicy hot chicken and prune baguettes

Serves 4
125g (4oz) cooked chicken
125g (4oz) ready-to-eat prunes
½ red onion, peeled and finely sliced
4 handfuls of rocket leaves
squeeze of lime juice
4 submarine rolls
freshly ground black pepper

For the curried mayonnaise
6 tbsp light mayonnaise
6 tbsp Greek yogurt
2 heaped tsp Thai red curry paste

1 Tear the chicken into strips and cut the prunes into bite-sized pieces.
2 Mix the ingredients for the curried mayonnaise together in a bowl. Add the chicken and prunes, mix well and season with pepper to taste.
3 In another bowl, toss the red onion with the rocket leaves and a good squeeze of lime juice.
4 Split the submarine rolls and toast, cut-side down, on a hot non-stick griddle pan. Sandwich together with the curried chicken mixture and rocket salad to serve.

Chicken strips and juicy prunes are tossed in a light Thai curry flavoured mayonnaise, then sandwiched in toasted submarine rolls with a rocket salad.

Mediterranean-style chicken salad

Serves 4

175g (6oz) cooked chicken breast

½ cucumber, halved, deseeded and
  chopped

6 small vine tomatoes, quartered

1 red onion, peeled and thinly sliced

20 black olives, pitted

20g (¾oz) flat leaf parsley, roughly
  chopped

For the dressing

2 tbsp extra virgin olive oil

3 garlic cloves, peeled and crushed

juice of 1 lemon

freshly ground black pepper

To serve

3 white pitta breads

1 Tear the cooked chicken into bite-sized pieces and place in a bowl with the
cucumber, tomatoes, red onion, olives and chopped parsley. Toss to mix.

2 For the dressing, whisk the olive oil with the garlic, lemon juice and
pepper to taste. Pour over the salad and toss gently.

3 Split the pitta breads and toast on both sides until crisp. Break the crispy
pittas over the salad and toss lightly to serve.

Another great way to create a healthy lunch
using chicken leftover from a roast.

Hot sesame chicken and avocado salad

Illustrated on previous pages

Serves 4

2 large skinless chicken breast fillets

3 tbsp wholegrain mustard

1 tbsp thin honey

juice of 1 lemon

½ tbsp sunflower oil

1 ripe avocado, stoned, peeled and
  sliced

large handful of crisp salad leaves,
  such as Little Gem lettuce

2 tbsp sesame seeds

1 tsp sesame oil

freshly ground black pepper

1 Cut the chicken breasts into finger-sized strips and place in a bowl. Season with black pepper and add the mustard, honey and lemon juice. Toss the chicken to mix well.

2 Heat the sunflower oil in a non-stick wok or large non-stick frying pan until very hot. Add the chicken mixture and stir-fry for 5–6 minutes or until golden and cooked. Meanwhile, toss the avocado slices with the salad leaves and pile on to four large plates.

3 Add the sesame seeds to the chicken and cook for a further 1 minute or until the seeds are just beginning to colour. Spoon the hot sesame chicken on top of the salad leaves and drizzle with the sesame oil. Serve at once as a light lunch or supper, with warm Granary bread to mop up the juices.

Packed with flavour, this quick and easy dish includes avocado. Regarded as a 'super food', avocado contains more protein than any other fruit, lots of vitamin E and useful potassium. It is also rich in monounsaturated fatty acids, which provide energy and help to maintain a healthy heart.

Thai green turkey burgers

Serves 4

450g (1lb) lean turkey mince

125g (4oz) grated carrot (3 medium carrots)

4 spring onions, trimmed and chopped

1½ tbsp Thai green curry paste

1 small egg white

1 tbsp groundnut oil

To serve

4 ciabatta rolls

handful of crisp salad leaves, such as rocket

4 cherry tomatoes, sliced

mango chutney, to taste

1 In a large bowl, mix the turkey mince with the grated carrot, spring onions and Thai green curry paste. Add the egg white and stir well to combine.

2 Divide the turkey mixture into four equal portions and shape into burgers. Place on a small board or flat plate, cover with cling film and chill in the refrigerator for 20 minutes.

3 Heat the groundnut oil in a large non-stick frying pan. Add the turkey burgers and cook for 5–7 minutes on each side or until golden brown on both sides and cooked through.

4 Split the ciabatta rolls. Serve the burgers in the rolls with crisp salad leaves, cherry tomato slices and a good spoonful of mango chutney.

These low fat, high protein burgers are spiced with Thai green curry paste and contain sweet grated carrot to keep them moist.

Turkey steaks with zesty gremolata

Serves 4

4 turkey steaks, each about
   125g (4oz)
grated zest and juice of 1 lemon
1 tbsp olive oil
1 ready-to-bake ciabatta roll,
   coarsely grated
1 garlic clove, peeled and finely
   chopped
20g (¾oz) flat leaf parsley, chopped
freshly ground black pepper

For the roasted beans and tomatoes

250g (9oz) baby plum tomatoes
250g (9oz) fine green beans,
   trimmed
1 tbsp olive oil

1 Preheat the oven to 200°C (fan oven 180°C), gas mark 6. Place each turkey steak between two pieces of cling film or greaseproof paper and beat to a 5mm (¼ inch) thickness, using a rolling pin. Lay the turkey steaks in a shallow ovenproof dish and sprinkle with the lemon juice and olive oil. Season with pepper.

2 Place the baby plum tomatoes and green beans on a roasting tray, drizzle over the olive oil and season with pepper. Scatter the ciabatta breadcrumbs on another small roasting tray.

3 Place both roasting trays into the oven. Remove the breadcrumbs after 5 minutes; they will be crisp and golden. Continue to cook the beans and tomatoes for a further 8–10 minutes.

4 Meanwhile, heat a non-stick ridged griddle pan until very hot. Add the turkey steaks and cook for 2–3 minutes on each side. (You may have to do this in two batches.)

5 Toss the toasted crumbs, lemon zest, garlic and parsley together in a bowl and season with pepper. Place the turkey steaks on warm serving plates, spoon over the roasted beans and tomatoes, then finish with a generous scattering of gremolata crumbs. Serve at once.

Aromatic turkey pilaf

Serves 4

300g (11oz) turkey breast fillet
225g (8oz) bulghar wheat, rinsed
1 tbsp sunflower oil
1 large onion, peeled and chopped
1 garlic clove, peeled and crushed
1½ tbsp garam masala
125g (4oz) ready-to-eat dried
  apricots, chopped
125g (4oz) sultanas
1 bay leaf
2 large carrots, peeled and coarsely
  grated
600ml–750ml (1–1¼ pints) chicken
  stock
4 tbsp chopped coriander
freshly ground black pepper
1 large lemon, cut into wedges, to
  serve

1 Cut the turkey into 1cm (½ inch) slices and set aside. Put the bulghar wheat in a bowl and add enough cold water to cover generously. Leave to stand for 15 minutes.

2 Meanwhile, heat the sunflower oil in a large non-stick sauté pan or non-stick wok, add the onion and cook for 5 minutes until softened. Increase the heat and add the turkey. Fry, turning frequently, for 3–4 minutes or until the turkey is golden all over. Stir in the garlic and garam masala, and cook for a further 1 minute.

3 Add the dried fruits, bay leaf and grated carrots, then pour in 600ml (1 pint) stock. Drain the bulghar wheat and add to the pan. Season with black pepper. Cover and cook gently for 15 minutes. Add extra stock if the pilaf becomes too dry; it should have the consistency of a risotto.

4 Spoon the pilaf into a large serving dish and stir in the coriander, reserving 1 tbsp to scatter over the top. Serve with the lemon wedges.

Bulghar wheat, or cracked bulghar wheat, has a good texture and a delicious nutty taste. In this pilaf it takes the place of rice, and carrots make a healthy addition You can replace the turkey with chicken or lean pork if you like.

healthy
meat

Lamb steaks with beet and spinach salad

Serves 4

4 lamb leg steaks, each about
   140g (4½oz)
2 garlic cloves, peeled and crushed
2 tbsp balsamic vinegar
1 tbsp olive oil
150g (5oz) baby leaf spinach
400g can butter beans, drained and
   rinsed
1 red onion, peeled and thinly sliced

250g (9oz) fresh baby beetroot,
   cooked and peeled
freshly ground black pepper
mint leaves, to serve

For the dressing

1 tbsp olive oil
1 tbsp white wine vinegar
1 tsp Dijon mustard
pinch of sugar
4 tbsp chopped mint

1 Place the lamb steaks in a non-metallic bowl. Add the garlic, balsamic vinegar, olive oil and plenty of black pepper. Turn the lamb steaks in the marinade to coat well, then set aside for 20 minutes, or longer in the refrigerator if possible.

2 To make the dressing, whisk the olive oil, wine vinegar, mustard, sugar and mint together in a large bowl. Season with a little pepper and set aside.

3 Heat a non-stick griddle pan over a medium-high heat. Add the lamb and cook for 2–3 minutes on each side for medium-rare, or longer to your liking. Pour in the marinade and allow to bubble and reduce to a glaze for the lamb.

4 Meanwhile, add the spinach, butter beans and red onion to the dressing and toss gently to combine. Divide the salad between four large serving plates and top with the baby beetroot. Place the lamb steaks alongside, spoon over the pan juices and scatter with a few mint leaves to serve.

Lean lamb steaks are griddled and served with a salad of baby spinach, butter beans and baby beetroot in a fresh minty dressing.

Babotie burgers

Illustrated on previous pages

Serves 4 (or 8)
4 tsp olive oil
1 large onion, peeled and finely
 chopped
1 tbsp garam masala
1 tsp ground cinnamon
450g (1lb) lean lamb mince
1 large carrot, peeled and grated
50g (2oz) fresh white breadcrumbs
50g (2oz) chopped almonds
grated zest of 1 lemon
1 egg, beaten
freshly ground black pepper

For the chutney
50g (2oz) sultanas
2 Cox's apples, diced
1 tbsp hot (spicy) mango chutney
seeds of 6 cardamom pods, crushed
2 tbsp chopped mint

1 Preheat the oven to 180°C (fan oven 160°C), gas mark 4. Heat 2 tsp olive oil in a pan and gently fry the onion for 10 minutes until soft and golden. Add the garam masala and cinnamon and cook for a further 1 minute. Tip into a large bowl and allow to cool.

2 Add the lamb mince, grated carrot, breadcrumbs, almonds and lemon zest to the cooled spiced onion and mix well. Season with pepper and add the beaten egg to bind the mixture.

3 Divide the mixture into eight portions. Roll into balls, then flatten to make small burgers. Heat the remaining olive oil in a large non-stick frying pan and sear the burgers quickly on each side.

4 Place the seared burgers on a non-stick baking tray and bake in the oven for 10–15 minutes or until cooked through. Meanwhile, mix all the ingredients for the chutney together and season to taste. Serve the burgers with the fruit chutney, crusty bread and a leafy salad.

There's nothing better than a real homemade burger and these spiced South African lamb burgers are particularly good. A fruity apple and mango chutney is the ideal complement.

Lamb and parsnip ragout

Illustrated on previous pages

Serves 4

350g (12oz) lean leg of lamb
1 tbsp plain flour
1 tbsp olive oil
1 onion, peeled and finely chopped
150g (5oz) baby carrots, scrubbed
2 parsnips, peeled and cut into
  chunks
2 bay leaves
2 tbsp sun-dried tomato paste
300ml (½ pint) red wine
450ml (¾ pint) vegetable stock
freshly ground black pepper
2 tbsp torn basil leaves, to sprinkle

For the garlic gnocchi

225g (8oz) plain flour
1 tsp baking powder
2 garlic cloves, peeled and crushed
2 tbsp olive oil
125ml (4fl oz) milk

1 Cut the lamb into 2cm (¾ inch) chunks and toss in the seasoned flour. Heat the olive oil in a large shallow, heavy-based pan and fry the lamb over a high heat until browned all over. Remove with a slotted spoon and set aside.

2 Add 2 tbsp water and the onion to the pan. Stir well over a medium heat, scraping up the crusty golden bits from the bottom of the pan. Lower the heat, cover and steam-fry for 5 minutes, stirring occasionally.

3 Stir in the carrots, parsnips and bay leaves and cook for 2 minutes, then return the lamb to the pan. Stir in the tomato paste, red wine and stock. Bring to the boil, cover and simmer for 25–30 minutes or until the lamb and vegetables are just tender.

4 To make the gnocchi, sift the flour and baking powder into a bowl and season well. Make a well in the middle. Combine the garlic, olive oil and milk, then add to the well and gradually incorporate the flour to make a soft, but not sticky, dough.

5 Shape the dough into 16 balls and place on top of the ragout. Replace the lid and simmer for a further 10 minutes. Scatter over the basil to serve.

Lamb with nectarine and cumin cous cous

Serves 4

4 lamb neck fillets, each about
   140g (4½oz)
2 tsp olive oil
freshly cracked black pepper
225g (8oz) cous cous
3 tbsp extra virgin olive oil

juice of 1 lemon
2 tsp cumin seeds, toasted
2 nectarines, halved, stoned and
   chopped
20g (¾oz) coriander, chopped
freshly ground black pepper

1 Brush the lamb neck fillets with the olive oil and roll in cracked pepper; set aside.

2 Put the cous cous in a bowl, pour on 250ml (8fl oz) boiling water and leave to soak for 5 minutes. Add the extra virgin olive oil, lemon juice, some pepper and the toasted cumin seeds, and fork through to combine. Add the chopped nectarines and coriander, toss gently to mix and set aside.

3 Heat a non-stick griddle pan until smoking. Add the lamb fillets and cook for about 6 minutes, turning to brown evenly. Remove from the pan and allow to rest for 5 minutes.

4 Slice the lamb thinly and serve with the fruity cous cous.

Gingered beef curry

Serves 4

2 sirloin steaks, each about
  250g (9oz)
1 tbsp olive oil
2 onions, peeled and sliced
2 tbsp Madras curry paste
5cm (2 inch) piece fresh root ginger,
  peeled and grated

600ml (1 pint) vegetable stock
400g can chick peas, drained and
  rinsed
100g (3½oz) spring greens, finely
  shredded
freshly coarse ground black pepper

1 Brush the steaks with a little olive oil and sprinkle with coarsely ground
black pepper. Heat a non-stick griddle pan until very hot. Add the steaks
to the griddle pan and sear for 2 minutes on each side for medium rare, or
1–2 minutes longer according to taste. Set aside to rest.
2 Heat the remaining olive oil in a large shallow pan, add the onions and
cook over a gentle heat for 5 minutes until beginning to soften. Add the
curry paste to the pan and stir well. Cover and steam-fry for 5 minutes over
a medium heat, stirring occasionally. Stir in the ginger and cook for
2 minutes.
3 Add the stock and chick peas to the pan, stir well and bring to the boil.
Simmer for 10 minutes. Stir in the spring greens, cover and cook for a
further 1 minute.
4 Slice the steaks into thin strips on the diagonal and stir into the curry.
Heat through for 1 minute and season to taste before serving. Serve with
basmati rice or chapattis.

A light, quick curry, cooked in a novel way.
Chick peas soak up the spicy curry flavours
and juicy griddled steak strips are added with
shredded spring greens at the end.

Sticky beef and pak choi stir-fry

Serves 4

225g (8oz) sirloin steak
250g (9oz) fine egg noodles
2 tsp groundnut oil
1 bunch of spring onions, trimmed
    and finely chopped

2 red peppers, deseeded and chopped
2 garlic cloves, peeled and crushed
300g (11oz) pak choi, shredded
4 tbsp plum sauce
2 tbsp dry sherry
2 tsp sesame oil

1 Cut the steak into strips and set aside. Cook the egg noodles in boiling water according to the packet instructions.
2 Meanwhile, heat the groundnut oil in a non-stick wok, add the steak strips and stir-fry over a high heat for 2 minutes. Add the spring onions, red peppers, garlic and pak choi and stir-fry for 1 minute. Stir in the plum sauce and sherry and cook for 1 minute.
3 Drain the noodles and toss with the sesame oil. Serve the peppered beef with the hot noodles.

Combining good quality lean steak with lots of vegetables in a stir-fry makes a little meat go a long way to create a healthy supper.

Fillet steak salad with wasabi dressing

Serves 4

4 red onions, peeled and cut into
  wedges
2 tbsp olive oil
225g (8oz) end of tail beef fillet
400g can green lentils, drained and
  rinsed
250g (9oz) watercress, trimmed
freshly ground black pepper

For the wasabi dressing

1 tbsp wasabi paste
7 tbsp natural yogurt

1 Preheat the oven to 200°C (fan oven 180°C), gas mark 6. Toss the onion wedges in 1 tbsp olive oil in a roasting tin and roast for 35 minutes.
2 Heat a non-stick griddle pan until it is smoking hot, then add the beef fillet and sear all over for 4–5 minutes or to taste. Remove from the pan and allow to rest for 5 minutes.
3 Meanwhile, toss the roasted onions with the lentils, watercress and remaining 1 tbsp olive oil. Season with pepper to taste. Divide between serving plates.
4 Mix the wasabi paste with the yogurt. Thinly slice the steak and arrange on the salad. Top with the wasabi dressing and serve.

Lean beef is a good source of easily absorbed iron and is also rich in zinc. Always let steak rest before cutting, as this allows the juices to be re-absorbed and keeps the meat succulent.

Chilli con carne pie

Serves 4–6

1 tbsp olive oil

1 onion, peeled and finely chopped

1 garlic clove, peeled and crushed

250g (9oz) lean steak mince

2 red chillies, deseeded and finely
  chopped

1 tsp ground cumin

1 tbsp red pepper tapenade

400g can chopped tomatoes

300ml (½ pint) vegetable stock

100g (3½oz) Puy lentils

400g can kidney beans, drained and
  rinsed

15g (½oz) plain dark chocolate,
  roughly chopped

freshly ground black pepper

For the mash

900g (2lb) white floury potatoes,
  such as Maris Piper, peeled

3 tbsp hot semi-skimmed milk

1 tsp ground turmeric

2 tbsp chopped coriander

1 Heat the olive oil in a large pan, add the onion and garlic and cook for
5 minutes. Turn up the heat, add the mince and cook, stirring, for 3 minutes
or until browned. Stir in the chillies and cumin and cook for 1 minute.

2 Add the tapenade, chopped tomatoes, stock, lentils and kidney beans, then
bring to the boil. Simmer for 25–30 minutes. Stir in the chocolate and season
with black pepper.

3 Meanwhile for the mash, cut the potatoes into even-sized chunks, add to a
pan of cold water and bring to the boil. Simmer for 20 minutes or until
tender, then drain. Tip the potatoes back into the pan and mash over a low
heat, stirring in the milk, turmeric and coriander. Season to taste.

4 Preheat the grill. Spoon the hot chilli beef into a gratin dish and spread
the hot mashed potato roughly over the top. Place under the grill for
5 minutes or until the topping is crisp and golden brown.

You can make this chilli as hot as you like.
I've used less meat than is usual, and added
Puy lentils and beans. The flavoured potato
crust makes a tasty change from boiled rice.

Steak and mushroom ciabattas

Serves 4

2 very large field mushrooms
4 tsp olive oil
300g (11oz) sirloin steak
1 tsp Worcestershire sauce
4 ready-to-bake ciabatta rolls, cooked
  according to packet instructions
85g packet watercress
freshly ground black pepper

For the mustard sauce

2 tbsp half-fat crème fraîche
1 tbsp Dijon mustard
1 tbsp wholegrain mustard

1 Preheat the grill to medium. Brush the mushrooms with 1 tbsp olive oil and season with pepper. Grill for 6 minutes on each side or until just cooked.
2 To make the sauce, mix the crème fraîche with the Dijon and wholegrain mustards in a small bowl until evenly blended and set aside.
3 Preheat a non-stick griddle pan until very hot. Brush the steak with the Worcestershire sauce and remaining olive oil, then season with pepper. Place on the griddle pan and sear for 2–3 minutes on each side or until cooked to your liking. Remove to a warm plate, cover loosely with foil and leave to rest for 5 minutes.
4 Cut each ciabatta roll in half and toast the cut sides under the grill for 1–2 minutes. Thinly slice the steak and mushrooms on the diagonal. Place the watercress on the bottom half of each roll and top with the steak and mushroom slices. Drizzle over the mustard sauce and cover with the lid of the roll. Serve immediately.

Char-grilled steak strips are served in a toasted ciabatta roll with field mushrooms, peppery watercress and a creamy mustard sauce for a satisfying supper or lunch.

Gammon with baby corn and pineapple

Serves 4

4 gammon steaks or pork loin
  steaks, each about 150g (5oz)
juice of 2 oranges
1 tbsp thin honey
½ bunch of spring onions, trimmed
  and finely chopped

1 small pineapple
200g (7oz) baby corn
2 tsp olive oil
1 red chilli, deseeded and finely
  chopped
freshly ground black pepper

1 Place the gammon steaks in a non-metallic dish, drizzle over the orange juice and honey, then add the spring onions and season well with black pepper. Set aside for 15 minutes.

2 Cut away the skin from the pineapple, then quarter and remove the core from each wedge. Heat a non-stick griddle pan until really hot. Cook the pineapple wedges and baby corn for 2 minutes each side or until slightly charred on the outside. Remove from the pan and keep warm.

3 Heat the olive oil in the griddle pan. Remove the gammon steaks from the marinade, reserving the liquid, and add to the pan. Cook for 3–4 minutes on each side, then transfer to warm serving plates.

4 Pour the reserved marinade into the pan and allow to bubble over a medium heat for 1 minute. Stir in the chilli and season to taste. Arrange the pineapple and baby corn alongside the gammon. Drizzle the hot dressing over and serve straightaway.

Here is a healthy, fresh twist to an old favourite. Lean gammon steaks are marinated in honey and orange juice, then char-grilled and served with griddled fresh pineapple and baby corn.

Pork meatballs with smoked goulash sauce

Illustrated on previous pages

Serves 4

350g (12oz) lean pork mince

100g (3½oz) carrot, peeled and grated

finely grated zest of 2 lemons

50g (2oz) sun-dried tomatoes, diced

2 tbsp chopped chives

75g (3oz) fresh white breadcrumbs

1 medium egg white

freshly ground black pepper

For the smoked goulash sauce

1 tbsp olive oil

2 aubergines, trimmed and diced

2 tsp smoked paprika

350g (12oz) tub fresh tomato sauce

200ml (7fl oz) red wine

1 Preheat the oven to 200°C (fan oven 180°C), gas mark 6. In a bowl, combine the pork mince with the grated carrot, lemon zest, sun-dried tomatoes, chives, breadcrumbs and some pepper, mixing thoroughly. Add the egg white to bind the mixture, then shape into 12 balls. Place on a non-stick baking tray and bake for 20 minutes.

2 Meanwhile, make the sauce. Heat the olive oil in a frying pan and sauté the aubergines for 5 minutes. Add the paprika and cook for 30 seconds. Stir in the tomato sauce and red wine, bring to the boil, then lower the heat and simmer for 5 minutes.

3 Serve the meatballs with the smoked goulash sauce.

Make your own meatballs, flavour them with fresh vegetables and serve in a tasty sauce for a healthy supper that's guaranteed to satisfy.

Pork and prune tagine style

Serves 4

450g (1lb) pork tenderloin, trimmed
2 tbsp harissa paste
1 tbsp olive oil
450ml (¾ pint) vegetable stock
1 onion, peeled and thinly sliced
grated zest and juice of 1 orange

4 carrots, peeled and cut into
   chunks on the diagonal
175g (6oz) ready-to-eat prunes
1 cinnamon stick
2 tbsp chopped coriander leaves
freshly ground black pepper

1 Cut the pork tenderloin into 1cm (½ inch) rounds and place in a bowl. Add the harissa paste and toss well to coat evenly.

2 Heat the olive oil in a large shallow pan, add the pork slices and cook for 1 minute on each side or until coloured. Remove with a slotted spoon and set aside.

3 Add 4 tbsp of the stock and the onion to the pan, cover and steam-fry over a medium heat for 5 minutes, stirring occasionally, until softened and golden.

4 Stir in the orange zest and juice, together with the remaining stock. Return the pork to the pan and add the carrots, prunes and cinnamon stick. Bring to the boil, then lower the heat and simmer for 15–20 minutes.

5 Season to taste with black pepper and scatter over chopped coriander leaves. Serve the tagine with cous cous or basmati rice.

Carrots and prunes give this Moroccan style dish a hint of sweetness and added nutrients. Carrots are rich in beta-carotene, while prunes are a good source of potassium, iron and fibre.

Red Thai pork with green beans

Serves 4

2 tsp olive oil

1 red onion, peeled and finely chopped

225g (8oz) pork tenderloin

2 tbsp Thai red curry paste

500g carton passata

1 tsp sugar

350g (12oz) French beans, topped and tailed

freshly ground black pepper

coriander or small basil leaves, to garnish

1 Heat the olive oil in a large shallow pan, add the chopped red onion and cook over a gentle heat for 10 minutes until soft and golden.

2 Meanwhile, cut the pork into 5mm (¼ inch) pieces. Turn up the heat under the pan to high, add the pork and cook, stirring, for 2 minutes until evenly coloured.

3 Stir in the Thai curry paste and cook for 1 minute. Pour in the passata, add the sugar and stir well. Bring to the boil, lower the heat and gently simmer for 8 minutes.

4 Meanwhile, blanch the French beans in boiling water for 1 minute, then drain and refresh under cold water; drain again and cut into short lengths. Add the beans to the curry and cook for a further 1 minute.

5 Season with pepper to taste. Scatter coriander or basil leaves over the curry and serve accompanied by Thai fragrant rice, and yogurt if you like.

For this simple aromatic curry, lean pork tenderloin is flavoured with Thai red curry paste and cooked in tomato passata with French beans. Serve with Thai fragrant rice, and a good dollop of cooling natural yogurt.

These spiced, lean pork skewers are served on a mouthwatering salad of roasted peppers and rocket, with a piquant sauce. Red peppers are one of the best sources of vitamin C.

Pork koftas with roasted pepper salad

Illustrated on previous pages

Serves 4

3 large red peppers, halved, cored
and deseeded
2 tbsp olive oil
1 onion, peeled and finely chopped
1 tsp cayenne pepper
2 tsp ground cumin
2 tsp ground coriander
450g (1lb) lean pork mince
1 egg white
½ bunch of flat leaf parsley, roughly
chopped
100g (3½oz) rocket leaves
freshly ground black pepper

For the sauce

200g (7oz) Greek yogurt
1 garlic clove, peeled and crushed
50g (2oz) black and green olives,
pitted and chopped
½ bunch of flat leaf parsley, roughly
chopped
squeeze of lemon juice

1 Preheat the oven to 200°C (fan oven 180°C), gas mark 6. Cut each pepper
half into 4 strips, place on a roasting tray and drizzle with 1 tbsp oil. Roast
for 35–40 minutes until softened and lightly charred.
2 Meanwhile, heat the remaining olive oil in a pan. Add the onion and cook
for 5–6 minutes until softened. Add the spices and cook for a further
1 minute. Transfer to a large bowl and allow to cool for 5 minutes. Add the
pork mince, egg white, parsley and plenty of black pepper. Mix thoroughly.
3 Preheat the grill to medium-high. Divide the pork mixture into eight and
shape each into a thick sausage. Push the sharp end of a pre-soaked bamboo
skewer through the length of each sausage and place on a grill pan. Grill
the koftas for about 6 minutes, turning occasionally, until cooked through.
4 Meanwhile, combine the sauce ingredients in a bowl; season with pepper.
Toss the roasted peppers with the rocket and divide between four plates. Top
with the koftas, add a spoonful of sauce and serve.

healthy
pasta and
rice

Tagliatelle with roast tomato and olive sauce

Serves 4

250g (9oz) cherry tomatoes

250g (9oz) baby plum tomatoes

175g (6oz) black olives, pitted and sliced

175g (6oz) green olives, pitted and sliced

pinch of sugar

2 tbsp olive oil

350g (12oz) dried tagliatelle

2 tbsp chopped flat leaf parsley

freshly ground black pepper

1 Preheat the oven to 200°C (fan oven 180°C), gas mark 6. Put the cherry and baby plum tomatoes into a roasting tin. Add the sliced olives, sugar, olive oil and plenty of pepper. Toss to mix, then roast for 20–25 minutes.

2 Ten minutes before the tomatoes will be ready, cook the tagliatelle in a large pan of boiling water until al dente (tender but firm to the bite).

3 Drain the pasta well and toss with the roasted tomato sauce and chopped parsley, mixing in all the pan juices. Serve at once.

Endlessly versatile, pasta is a great energy food – high in beneficial carbohydrate, low in fat and a useful source of protein – and it's not fattening unless you dress it to be so.

Roasted butternut farfalle

Serves 4

1 large butternut squash, peeled, halved and deseeded

2 large red onions, peeled and cut into thin wedges

2 tbsp olive oil

350g (12oz) dried farfalle, or other pasta shapes

50g (2oz) pine nuts, lightly toasted

50g (2oz) wild rocket

freshly ground black pepper

balsamic vinegar, to drizzle

1 Preheat the oven to 200°C (fan oven 180°C), gas mark 6. Cut the butternut squash into 2.5cm (1 inch) pieces and place in a large roasting tin with the red onions. Drizzle with the olive oil and season with black pepper. Roast for 40–45 minutes until the vegetables are tender and slightly caramelised.

2 About 10 minutes before the end of the roasting time, cook the pasta in a large pan of boiling water according to the packet instructions, until al dente (tender but firm to the bite).

3 Drain the pasta, reserving 2 tbsp of the cooking water, then return to the pan. Add the roasted vegetables, pine nuts and rocket with the reserved water. Toss to mix and season with plenty of black pepper. Pile on to warm serving plates, drizzle with a little balsamic vinegar and serve.

Roasted butternut squash and red onions are teamed with rocket, pasta and pine nuts for a simple, stunning meal. Winter squash, such as butternut, are a useful source of vitamin A.

Rigatoni with chillied tenderstem broccoli

Serves 4

350g (12oz) dried rigatoni or penne
350g (12oz) long-stemmed broccoli,
    trimmed and cut into long florets
2 red chillies, deseeded and finely
    diced
 squeeze of lemon juice
2 tbsp extra virgin olive oil
freshly ground black pepper

1 Cook the pasta in a large pan of boiling water for 8–10 minutes or until
al dente (tender but firm to the bite).
2 Meanwhile, steam the broccoli for 4 minutes or until al dente.
3 Drain the cooked pasta and toss with the broccoli, chillies, lemon juice and
extra virgin olive oil. Grind over lots of black pepper and serve straightaway.

Broccoli is an excellent source of vitamin C
and antioxidants that may help to reduce the
risk of certain cancers.

This is an unusual way of serving spaghetti. Canned tuna is an excellent source of protein and a good storecupboard standby. Tuna canned in spring water is a healthier option than fish in oil or brine.

Spaghetti rosti with tuna

Illustrated on previous pages

Serves 4–6
225g (8oz) dried spaghetti
1 tbsp olive oil
1 onion, peeled and finely chopped
1 garlic clove, peeled and crushed
5 eggs, beaten
2 x 160g cans yellow fin tuna in
    spring water, drained and flaked
40g (1½oz) mature Cheddar cheese,
    grated
freshly ground black pepper

1 Cook the spaghetti in a large pan of boiling water for 8–10 minutes or until al dente (tender but firm to the bite). Drain, rinse under cold running water, drain well and place in a large bowl.
2 Meanwhile, heat the olive oil in a large non-stick frying pan (suitable for use under the grill). Add the onion and cook for 5 minutes, then stir in the garlic and cook for a further 1 minute. Add to the cooked pasta with the beaten eggs and tuna and toss to mix, seasoning well.
3 Preheat the grill. Arrange the spaghetti mixture evenly in the frying pan and scatter over the cheese. Continue to cook on the hob for 10 minutes or until the eggs are almost set.
4 Place under the grill for 3–4 minutes or until just set and golden on top. Slide the rosti out of the pan on to a board. Cut into wedges and serve warm with roasted vine tomatoes or salad leaves. Alternatively, allow to cool and pack into lunchboxes.

Lemon and haddock penne bake

Serves 4

300g (11oz) dried penne or other
  pasta shapes
250g (9oz) broccoli florets
450g (1lb) natural smoked haddock
  fillet
450ml (¾ pint) semi-skimmed milk

25g (1oz) butter
1 tbsp plain flour
grated zest and juice of ½ lemon
40g (1½oz) mature Cheddar cheese,
  grated
5 tbsp fresh white breadcrumbs
freshly ground black pepper

1 Preheat the oven to 200°C (fan oven 180°C), gas mark 6. Cook the pasta in
a large pan of boiling water according to the packet instructions, until
al dente (tender but firm to the bite). Blanch the broccoli florets in boiling
water for 2 minutes, then drain and refresh in cold water.
2 Place the smoked haddock fillet in a shallow pan, pour over the milk and
cover with a circle of greaseproof paper. Bring to a simmer and poach gently
for 3–4 minutes. Remove the smoked haddock to a plate, reserving the milk.
3 Melt the butter in a small pan, stir in the flour and cook over a gentle heat
for 2 minutes. Slowly whisk in the reserved milk and cook for 5 minutes.
Add the lemon zest and juice, and season the sauce with pepper to taste.
4 Drain the pasta as soon as it is cooked. Roughly flake the haddock and
mix with the pasta and broccoli florets. Place in a large gratin dish and pour
over the sauce.
5 Mix together the Cheddar cheese and breadcrumbs, then scatter over the
top. Bake in the oven for 10 minutes or until bubbling hot and golden. Serve
immediately, accompanied by a tomato salad.

Juicy flakes of natural smoked haddock,
penne pasta and broccoli are baked in a
creamy lemon sauce beneath a crispy, cheesy
crumb topping.

Boston bean and sausage macaroni

Serves 4

4 good quality sausages
175g (6oz) dried macaroni
500g carton passata
40g (1½oz) brown sugar
3 tbsp tomato ketchup
3 tbsp white wine vinegar
dash of Worcestershire sauce

400g can pinto beans, drained and
  rinsed
400g can haricot beans, drained and
  rinsed
good handful of rocket leaves
40g (1½oz) mature Cheddar cheese,
  pared into shavings
freshly ground black pepper

1 Preheat the oven to 200°C (fan oven 180°C), gas mark 6. Preheat the grill. Lay the sausages on the grill pan and grill for 12–15 minutes, turning frequently, until browned all over and cooked through.

2 Cook the macaroni in a large pan of boiling water according to the packet instructions, until al dente (tender but firm to the bite).

3 Meanwhile, place the passata, sugar, tomato ketchup, wine vinegar and Worcestershire sauce in a pan. Stir together, then add the pinto and haricot beans and simmer for 10 minutes.

4 Drain the macaroni and add to the beans. Cut each sausage into 4 chunky slices and stir into the bean mixture, then season to taste. Spoon into an ovenproof gratin dish and place in the oven for 8–10 minutes until piping hot. Just before serving, scatter over the rocket leaves and cheese shavings.

Make sure you use good quality sausages for this American style dish, as they'll be less fatty and more flavoursome.

Pasta with pea pesto, ricotta and cured ham

Serves 4

350g (12oz) dried pasta spirals

225g (8oz) frozen petit pois

5 tbsp basil leaves

125g (4oz) ricotta cheese

2 tsp lemon juice

1 garlic clove, peeled and crushed

4–6 wafer-thin slices of dry cured
    ham, roughly torn

freshly ground black pepper

basil leaves, to garnish

1 Cook the pasta spirals in a large pan of boiling water until al dente (tender but firm to the bite).

2 Meanwhile, cook the petit pois in boiling water for 3 minutes then drain, reserving 125ml (4fl oz) of the liquid.

3 Put the peas and reserved liquid into a food processor, add the basil, ricotta, lemon juice and garlic, and whiz until fairly smooth. Season with pepper to taste. Transfer the pea pesto to a small pan and warm gently.

4 Drain the pasta and toss with the pesto. Divide between warm bowls and scatter over the torn slices of dry cured ham. Garnish with basil and serve.

Petit pois are a must in the freezer as they are such a useful standby and provide vitamin C, which helps the body to absorb iron.

Moroccan dressed chick peas and pasta

Serves 4
2 tsp olive oil
1 red onion, peeled and thinly sliced
2 tbsp harissa paste
6 tbsp white wine

400g can chopped tomatoes
400g can chick peas, drained
350g (12oz) dried penne or other
 pasta shapes
freshly ground black pepper

1 Heat the olive oil in a pan, stir in the onion and steam-fry for 5 minutes. Stir in the harissa paste, white wine and chopped tomatoes. Bring to a simmer and cook gently for 10 minutes. Add the chick peas and heat through. Season with pepper to taste.
2 Meanwhile, cook the pasta in a large pan of boiling water for 8–10 minutes or until al dente (tender but firm to the bite).
3 Drain the pasta, return to the pan and add the tomato and chick pea sauce. Toss to mix and serve.

Keep tasting pasta towards the end of cooking. It's ready when it's al dente – firm to the tooth – not hard or chalky, and definitely not soggy.

Green rice soubise

Serves 4

1 tbsp olive oil

2 onions, peeled and finely chopped

2 garlic cloves, peeled and crushed

350g (12oz) short-grain American easy-cook brown rice, rinsed

1 unwaxed lemon, cut into 4 wedges

1.2 litres (2 pints) vegetable stock

250g (9oz) broccoli florets

175g (6oz) frozen peas, thawed

1 bunch of spring onions, trimmed and chopped

125g (4oz) ricotta cheese

2 tbsp torn basil

freshly ground black pepper

1 Preheat the oven to 200°C (fan oven 180°C), gas mark 6. Heat the olive oil in a large shallow ovenproof pan, add the onions and cook over a medium heat for 5 minutes, stirring occasionally. Add the garlic and cook for a further 2 minutes until the onions are softened and golden.

2 Add the rice and lemon wedges, then stir well. Pour in the stock, bring to the boil and cover with foil. Cook in the oven for 45–50 minutes. In the meantime, blanch the broccoli in boiling water for 2–3 minutes, then drain and refresh under cold running water.

3 Remove the rice dish from oven and stir in the broccoli, peas and spring onions. Season well and crumble the ricotta on top. Bake, uncovered, for a further 6–8 minutes or until the rice is tender and most of the liquid has been absorbed. Scatter over the basil and serve straightaway.

Wholemeal rice contains more fibre than white rice and takes longer to cook. Fortunately, this lemony wholemeal rice dish is baked, so once it's in the oven you can forget about it.

Oriental rice with shiitake mushrooms

Illustrated on previous pages

Serves 4

2 sachets instant miso soup powder

1 tbsp olive oil

5cm (2 inch) piece fresh root ginger, peeled and finely chopped

1 garlic clove, peeled and crushed

1 small red chilli, deseeded and finely chopped

½ bunch of spring onions, trimmed and chopped

225g (8oz) arborio rice

350g (12oz) sugar snap peas, trimmed

250g (9oz) shiitake mushrooms, sliced

2 tbsp Japanese furikake seasoning

2 tsp mirin

freshly ground black pepper

coriander sprigs, to garnish

1 Mix the miso powder with 900ml (1½ pints) boiling water in a saucepan and keep at a gentle simmer over a low heat.

2 Heat ½ tbsp olive oil in a pan over a medium heat, add the ginger, garlic, chilli and spring onions, and cook for 1 minute. Stir in the rice.

3 Keeping the rice over a medium heat, add the miso, a ladleful at a time, stirring constantly and making sure each addition is absorbed before adding more (this will take approximately 20 minutes). The rice is cooked when it looks thick and creamy, but still retains a bite. Season to taste.

4 Heat the remaining olive oil in a non-stick wok or large non-stick frying pan. Add the sugar snap peas and mushrooms and stir-fry for 2–3 minutes. Stir in the furikake seasoning and mirin, and cook for a further 30 seconds.

5 Spoon the rice into warm serving bowls and add the stir-fried sugar snaps and mushrooms. Garnish with coriander sprigs and serve immediately.

This sticky risotto, infused with Japanese flavours, is a tasty low-fat alternative to a traditional Italian risotto.

Red rice comes from the Camargue region in southern France. It has a good flavour, nutty texture and a distinctive colour. Peppers are a good source of beta-carotene, the plant form of vitamin A, which may help to reduce the risk of some forms of cancer and heart disease.

Jambalaya

Illustrated on previous pages

Serves 4

2 skinless chicken breast fillets,
  each about 150g (5oz)
1 each red, yellow and orange
  peppers
350g (12oz) Camargue red rice
80g packet sliced chorizo sausage
1 tbsp olive oil
1 red onion, peeled and cut into
  8 wedges

2 garlic cloves, peeled and crushed
1½ tsp smoked paprika
pinch of ground cloves
3 bay leaves
400g can chopped tomatoes
200ml (7fl oz) vegetable stock
freshly ground black pepper

1 Cut the chicken into 2.5cm (1 inch) pieces. Halve, core and deseed the peppers, then chop roughly. Cook the rice in a pan of boiling water according to the packet instructions.

2 Meanwhile, heat a large shallow pan, add the chorizo slices and cook for 30 seconds on each side until golden. Remove with a slotted spoon and set aside. Add the chicken pieces to the pan and sauté for 10 minutes until golden all over. Remove from the pan and drain on kitchen paper.

3 Add the olive oil to the pan. Add the red onion and peppers and cook for 5 minutes or until the vegetables are lightly golden. Stir in the garlic, smoked paprika, cloves and bay leaves. Cook for 1 minute.

4 Stir in the drained, cooked rice, chorizo and chicken. Add the tomatoes and stock, and bring to the boil. Simmer for 8–10 minutes or until most of the liquid has been absorbed. Season to taste and serve.

Baked chicken and thyme risotto

Serves 4

25g (1oz) dried porcini mushrooms
4 skinless chicken thigh fillets
2 garlic cloves, peeled and crushed
2 tsp thyme leaves, plus extra to
   garnish
1 tbsp olive oil
1 large onion, peeled and finely
   chopped
1 litre (1¾ pints) vegetable stock
350g (12oz) arborio rice
100ml (3½fl oz) white wine
freshly ground black pepper

1 Put the dried mushrooms in a bowl, pour over warm water to cover and leave to soak for about 30 minutes. Preheat the oven to 190°C (fan oven 170°C), gas mark 5.

2 With a small sharp knife, slash the chicken thighs on the diagonal, just cutting through the flesh. Rub them all over with the garlic and thyme, then season with pepper.

3 Heat the olive oil in a large shallow ovenproof pan and cook the chicken for 2–3 minutes on each side until golden. Remove and set aside.

4 Add the onion to the pan with a splash of stock and cook gently for about 5 minutes until softened. Stir in the rice and stir continuously for 1 minute. Add the drained mushrooms and cook for a further 1 minute. Pour in the wine and cook for 2 minutes until it has evaporated.

5 Add the stock and bring to the boil. Season well. Place the chicken thighs on top of the rice. Cover with a lid and cook in the oven for 20–25 minutes until the rice is just cooked and all the stock has been absorbed. Scatter over extra thyme leaves, then serve.

This oven-baked chicken risotto doesn't require constant stirring, but the result is still creamy and flavoursome. It is rich in protein, carbohydrates and wheat-free.

Crab and salmon kedgeree

Serves 4

2 tsp olive oil
1 onion, peeled and finely chopped
2 tbsp Thai green curry paste
2 tbsp mango chutney
150ml (¼ pint) white wine
300ml (½ pint) vegetable stock
350g (12oz) basmati rice, rinsed
350g (12oz) boneless, skinless
   salmon fillet
170g can white crabmeat, drained

For the raita

200g (7oz) natural yogurt
1 small carrot, peeled and grated
20g (¾oz) coriander leaves, chopped
freshly ground black pepper

1 Preheat the oven to 200°C (fan oven 180°C), gas mark 6. Heat the olive oil in a pan, stir in the onion and steam-fry for 10 minutes or until soft and golden. Stir in the curry paste and mango chutney and cook for 1 minute. Pour in the wine and stock, then cook until reduced to about 250ml (8fl oz).
2 Meanwhile, cook the rice according to the packet instructions. Cut the salmon into 8 strips lengthways and place on a non-stick baking tray. Bake in the oven for 5–7 minutes until just cooked.
3 Mix all the ingredients for the raita together in a bowl and season well with black pepper.
4 Drain the rice and gently toss with the reduced curry paste mixture, then fork through the crabmeat. Spoon the kedgeree on to warm serving plates, top with the salmon strips and serve immediately, with the carrot and coriander raita.

This kedgeree with a twist is surprisingly spiced with Thai green curry paste. Crab gives a deliciously different flavour, while roasted salmon strips provide an attractive topping.

healthy
salads and
vegetables

Cashew nut and rice noodle salad

Serves 4

50g (2oz) cashew nuts
2 medium carrots, peeled
20g (¾oz) coriander sprigs
2 tbsp light soy sauce
juice of 1 large orange
3 garlic cloves, peeled and crushed

2 tbsp grapeseed oil
250g (9oz) rice noodles, cooked
1 bunch of radishes, trimmed and
   sliced
125g (4oz) bean sprouts
freshly ground black pepper

1 Place the cashew nuts in a small dry frying pan over a medium heat and toast for about 3 minutes, shaking the pan constantly, until an even golden colour. Set aside to cool slightly.

2 Using a swivel vegetable peeler, pare along the length of the carrots to make long, thin ribbons and set aside.

3 Set aside a handful of coriander sprigs. Put the rest into a food processor with the toasted cashew nuts, soy sauce, orange juice, garlic and grapeseed oil. Whiz until fairly smooth, then season to taste.

4 Toss the noodles, carrot ribbons, radishes and bean sprouts together. Pour over the dressing and toss well to coat evenly. Scatter over the reserved coriander to serve.

These rice noodles are great for anyone on a wheat-free diet and they're so quick to cook. Cashew nuts provide protein, minerals – especially magnesium – and some B vitamins.

Tabbouleh is a fragrant Middle Eastern salad
made with nutty bulghar wheat, lemon juice,
olive oil and lots of fresh mint and parsley.
Here it is served with oven-roasted tomatoes,
spiked with harissa. Pine nuts are high in
essential fatty acids and provide added protein
to make this a complete meal for vegetarians.

Harissa tomatoes with tabbouleh

Illustrated on previous pages

Serves 4

225g (8oz) bulghar wheat
4 beefsteak tomatoes, halved
2 tbsp harissa paste
2 tbsp extra virgin olive oil, plus
   extra to drizzle
juice of 1 lemon
20g (¾oz) mint, chopped
20g (¾oz) flat leaf parsley, chopped
75g (3oz) pine nuts, toasted
freshly ground black pepper
natural yogurt, to serve

1 Preheat the oven to 220°C (fan oven 200°C), gas mark 7. Put the bulghar wheat in a bowl and add cold water to just cover. Set aside for 30 minutes or until the water has been absorbed.
2 Place the tomatoes, cut-side up, on a baking tray and spread with the harissa paste. Roast in the oven for 10–12 minutes or until just softened but still holding their shape.
3 Meanwhile, toss the bulghar wheat with the olive oil, lemon juice, chopped mint and parsley. Season to taste.
4 Spoon the tabbouleh on to four plates and top each serving with two roasted tomato halves. Scatter over the toasted pine nuts and drizzle with a little extra virgin olive oil. Serve with yogurt.

Guacamole and bean salad on toasted pitta

Serves 4

2 ripe avocados
juice of 1 lime
2 shallots, peeled and finely chopped
10 cherry tomatoes, quartered
1 red chilli, deseeded and finely
  chopped
2 garlic cloves, peeled and crushed

2 tbsp extra virgin olive oil
400g can kidney beans, drained and
  rinsed
75g (3oz) bag ready-prepared
  watercress
6 pitta breads, toasted
freshly ground black pepper

1 Halve, stone and peel the avocados, then cut into 1cm (½ inch) cubes. Place in a bowl and pour over the lime juice. Add the shallots, cherry tomatoes, chilli, 1 garlic clove and 1 tbsp olive oil, and gently mix together. Season with black pepper.

2 Toss the kidney beans with the remaining garlic and olive oil, then toss in the watercress and season well. Spoon on to toasted pitta breads and top with the chunky guacamole.

Chunky guacamole, made from nutrient-rich avocados, partners a Mexican-style bean and watercress salad that's rich in fibre and iron. Best serve with toasted pitta bread.

Warm peppered goat's cheese salad

Serves 4

2 x 100g (3½oz) goat's cheese with
  rind
1 tbsp freshly ground black pepper
2 tbsp cooked Puy lentils

1 small red pepper, deseeded and
  finely diced
3 tbsp extra virgin olive oil
juice of ½ lemon
150g (5oz) baby salad leaves

1 Cut each cheese in half horizontally and coat all over with the pepper, pressing to adhere. Heat a non-stick griddle pan until hot. Add the peppered cheese, cut-side down, and griddle for 2 minutes or until coloured and crusty. Turn over and cook for a further 1 minute or until the cheese is soft but still retaining its shape.

2 Meanwhile, mix together the lentils, red pepper, olive oil and lemon juice in a small bowl; season well. Arrange the salad leaves on serving plates, top with the griddled goat's cheese and spoon over the dressing to serve.

Goat's cheese has a sharp, gutsy flavour, so a little goes a long way. Here it's coated in black pepper, then griddled and served on salad leaves, drizzled with an unusual red pepper and lentil dressing.

Mango crab salad

Serves 4

1 Cos lettuce, trimmed
1 cucumber
1 small ripe mango
250g (9oz) fresh brown crabmeat
350g (12oz) fresh white crabmeat
1 lime, cut into wedges

For the dressing

3 tbsp low-fat mayonnaise
6 tbsp natural yogurt
2 tbsp hot lime pickle

1 Tear the Cos lettuce leaves into pieces. Peel, halve, deseed and slice the cucumber on the diagonal. Peel, halve and slice the mango away from the stone. Arrange these ingredients on a large platter, or individual plates.

2 Place a mound of brown crabmeat in the centre and top with the fresh white crabmeat. Mix the dressing ingredients together in a bowl.

3 Serve the crab salad with the lime pickle mayonnaise, lime wedges and some good brown bread.

This is a healthy salad with a difference. Mango is rich in vitamins C, A and E. Like all shellfish, crab is a good source of protein, B vitamins and some minerals, including zinc.

Hot new potato salad with smoked trout

Illustrated on previous pages

Serves 4

750g (1lb 10oz) baby new potatoes,
    scrubbed
1 tbsp olive oil
2 large handfuls lamb's lettuce
250g (9oz) cooked baby beetroot,
    halved
75g (3oz) smoked trout, flaked
freshly ground black pepper

For the dressing

2 tsp wholegrain mustard
1 tsp Dijon mustard
4 tbsp Greek yogurt
juice of ½ lemon
¼ tsp thin honey

1 Preheat the oven to 190°C (fan oven 170°C), gas mark 5. Toss the baby new potatoes with some black pepper and the olive oil in a roasting tin. Roast for 45 minutes or until tender.

2 Meanwhile, make the dressing. In a bowl, mix together the wholegrain and Dijon mustards, yogurt, lemon juice, honey and 1 tbsp water until combined.

3 Divide the lamb's lettuce, beetroot and smoked trout between plates and add the hot potatoes. Drizzle with the mustard dressing and serve.

Potatoes are rich in complex carbohydrate and contain useful amounts of fibre, vitamin C, potassium and protein. Some nutrients are concentrated just under the skin, so scrub rather than peel potatoes.

Warm potato and soft-boiled egg salad

Serves 4

575g (1¼lb) baby new potatoes, scrubbed
225g (8oz) green beans, trimmed and halved
250g (9oz) cherry tomatoes, halved
4 eggs
2 punnets mustard and cress, trimmed

For the dressing

2 tsp Dijon mustard
1 tbsp white wine vinegar
1 shallot, peeled and finely chopped
1 garlic clove, peeled and crushed
3 tbsp extra virgin olive oil
freshly ground black pepper

1 Place the baby new potatoes in a pan of cold water, bring to the boil and simmer for 20 minutes or until just tender.
2 Meanwhile, make the dressing. Whisk the Dijon mustard, wine vinegar, shallot, garlic and olive oil together in a bowl and season to taste.
3 Drain the potatoes and toss them in the dressing. Set aside to cool for 5 minutes. Blanch the green beans in boiling water for 1 minute, then drain and refresh under cold running water; drain well. Add the beans and tomatoes to the potatoes and toss to mix.
4 Meanwhile, place the eggs in a pan with enough boiling water to cover and boil gently for 2 minutes. Put the eggs under running cold water, then remove and very carefully peel them.
5 To serve, spoon the salad into bowls, top each serving with a soft-boiled egg and scatter over mustard and cress. Serve immediately.

This is a lovely fresh combination of colourful ingredients. Tossing the baby new potatoes in the mustard dressing while they are still hot encourages them to soak up all the flavours.

Griddled pear, chicken and endive salad

Illustrated on previous pages

Serves 4

2 large, ripe William or Comice pears
275g (10oz) cooked chicken breast
200g bag curly endive (frisé) and
  radicchio salad
50g (2oz) walnuts, toasted
50g (2oz) Roquefort cheese,
  crumbled

For the dressing

2 tbsp extra virgin olive oil
2 tbsp balsamic vinegar
freshly ground black pepper

1 Halve, quarter, core and thickly slice the pears. Heat a non-stick griddle pan until very hot. Add the pear slices and griddle for 1 minute on each side or until lightly charred. Remove and set aside.

2 For the dressing, whisk the olive oil and balsamic vinegar together in a small bowl. Season with pepper to taste.

3 Tear the chicken into bite-sized pieces. Arrange the salad leaves on four serving plates and top with the chicken, pears, toasted walnuts and crumbled blue cheese. Drizzle the dressing over the salad and grind over a little extra black pepper. Serve with Granary bread.

Griddled, sliced pears complement bitter salad leaves, tangy Roquefort and chicken to delicious effect. Chicken is rich in protein – buy organic or free-range for a healthy option.

Melon, roasted pepper and ham salad

Illustrated on previous pages

Serves 4
3 large orange peppers
2 tsp olive oil
1 small ripe Charentais or Galia
  melon
100g (3½oz) rocket leaves

125g (4oz) wafer-thin honey roast
  ham slices
50g (2oz) pecorino cheese, crumbled
extra virgin olive oil, to drizzle
freshly ground black pepper

1 Preheat the oven to 220°C (fan oven 200°C), gas mark 7. Quarter, core and deseed the peppers, then place in a roasting tin and drizzle with the olive oil. Roast for 20–25 minutes. Set aside to cool.
2 Cut the melon in half and scoop out the seeds, then cut each half into 4 wedges.
3 Arrange the rocket on serving plates and top with the melon, roasted peppers and ham. Scatter over the cheese and finish with a generous grinding of black pepper and a little drizzle of extra virgin olive oil.

A colourful salad of ripe, juicy melon, roasted peppers, honey roast ham, tangy pecorino and rocket leaves. An Italian sheep's milk cheese, pecorino is rich in protein and calcium.

Vegetable hash with eggs

Serves 4

450g (1lb) Maris Piper or King
   Edward potatoes, peeled
2 tbsp olive oil
2 leeks, trimmed and finely
   shredded
2 carrots, peeled and grated
4 small or medium eggs
1 tbsp chopped flat leaf parsley
freshly ground black pepper

1 Grate the potatoes, then squeeze out as much liquid as possible with your hands and pat dry on kitchen paper. Preheat the grill.

2 Heat the olive oil in a large 23–25cm (9–10 inch) non-stick frying pan (suitable for use under the grill). Add the leeks and cook, stirring, for 2 minutes. Stir in the grated potatoes and carrots, then lightly spread out the mixture in the pan. Fry over a medium heat for 10 minutes until golden and crisp underneath.

3 Place the pan under the grill and cook for 5 minutes or until the rosti is golden on top. Remove from the grill and make four indentations in the surface of the rosti.

4 Crack the eggs into the indentations, grind over a little black pepper and scatter over the chopped parsley. Cover with a lid or baking sheet, place back on the hob over a medium heat and cook for 4–5 minutes or until the eggs are cooked to your liking. Serve straightaway.

A mixed root vegetable rosti topped with protein-rich eggs makes an appetising, healthy lunch or supper. Always buy free-range or organic eggs for taste and quality.

Pak choi and noodle stir-fry

Serves 4

250g (9oz) thin egg noodles
2 tbsp groundnut oil
250g (9oz) small chestnut
    mushrooms, halved or quartered
    if large
2 garlic cloves, peeled and crushed

2 red chillies, deseeded and finely
    chopped
3 pak choi, shredded
2 tbsp soy sauce
2 tbsp sweet chilli dipping sauce
freshly ground black pepper
coriander sprigs, to garnish

1 Cook the egg noodles in boiling water according to the packet instructions.
2 At the same time, cook the stir-fry. Heat the groundnut oil in a non-stick wok or large non-stick frying pan. Add the mushrooms and garlic and stir-fry for 1–2 minutes. Stir in the chillies and cook for 30 seconds. Add the pak choi and stir-fry for 1 minute.
3 Toss in the drained egg noodles, soy and chilli sauces, and season with pepper to taste. Heat through for 1 minute or until the noodles are piping hot. Divide between warm bowls, garnish with coriander and serve at once.

Stir-frying is one of the healthiest ways of cooking vegetables as it helps to preserve their vitamin C – the least stable of all vitamins.

Roasted Mediterranean vegetable crust

Illustrated on previous pages

Serves 6

1 aubergine

2 courgettes, trimmed

2 red peppers, halved and deseeded

1 small red onion, peeled

150g (5oz) cherry tomatoes

2 tbsp olive oil

½ x 500g (1lb 2oz) packet ciabatta bread mix

50g (2oz) black olives, pitted and chopped

125g (4oz) feta cheese, crumbled

small handful of torn basil leaves

freshly ground black pepper

1 Preheat the oven to 220°C (fan oven 200°C), gas mark 7. Chop the aubergine, courgettes, peppers and onion into 1cm (½ inch) chunks and place in a roasting tin with the cherry tomatoes, in a single layer. Drizzle over the olive oil, season well with black pepper and roast for 25–30 minutes.

2 Meanwhile, make up the half quantity of ciabatta bread mix according to the packet instructions, using half the suggested quantity of water and adding the chopped black olives as you knead the dough. Set aside.

3 Transfer the roasted vegetables to a shallow, round non-stick baking tin or gratin dish, about 23cm (9 inches) in diameter. Roll out the olive dough to a round a little larger than the tin and place on top of the vegetables. Press the dough down well and to the side of the tin. Bake for 15–20 minutes.

4 Cool for a few minutes, then place a large serving plate over the tin, invert and carefully turn out the vegetable crust. Tap the tin to make sure all the vegetables come away. Scatter the feta and basil over the vegetables and cut into wedges to serve.

This impressive tart is easy to make, using a ciabatta bread mix. Roasted vegetables are baked under the dough, then inverted and topped with crumbled feta to serve. A sheep's milk cheese, feta is useful for anyone with an intolerance to cow's milk protein.

Butternut barley risi

Serves 4

125g (4oz) pearl barley, rinsed

1 large butternut squash, peeled and deseeded

2 tbsp olive oil

1 large leek, trimmed and finely sliced

1 garlic clove, peeled and chopped

2 bay leaves

2 large strips of orange peel

1.2 litres (2 pints) vegetable stock

4 tbsp chopped flat leaf parsley

freshly ground black pepper

freshly grated Parmesan cheese, to serve

1 Soak the pearl barley in cold water to cover for 30 minutes. Preheat the oven to 200°C (fan oven 180°C), gas mark 6.

2 Cut the butternut squash into 2.5 cm (1 inch) pieces, place on a large roasting tray, drizzle with 1 tbsp of the olive oil and season with pepper. Roast in the oven for 35–40 minutes until tender and slightly caramelised.

3 Meanwhile, heat the remaining olive oil in a large saucepan. Add the leek and garlic and steam-fry for 5 minutes until softened. Drain the pearl barley and add to the leek with the bay leaves, orange peel and stock. Bring to the boil and simmer gently for 30 minutes or until the barley is just tender.

4 Stir the parsley through the risi and season with black pepper to taste. Ladle into warm bowls or soup plates and top with the roasted butternut and Parmesan to serve.

Barley is an interesting, under-rated grain with a nutty texture. It is easily digested and highly nutritious, providing a good source of fibre, calcium and protein. It goes well with roasted butternut squash.

Sweet vegetable and coconut green curry

Serves 4

2 tsp olive oil
1 onion, peeled and finely chopped
2½ tbsp Thai green curry paste
3 medium sweet potatoes, peeled

400g can reduced-fat coconut milk
1 cinnamon stick
150g packet marinated tofu
200g (7oz) petit pois
2 tbsp chopped coriander leaves

1 Heat the olive oil in a pan. Add the onion and steam-fry for 5 minutes, then stir in the curry paste and cook for 1 minute.

2 Meanwhile, cut the sweet potatoes into 2.5cm (1 inch) chunks. Add to the spiced onion and stir to coat evenly in the mixture. Pour in the coconut milk and 150ml (¼ pint) water, and add the cinnamon stick. Bring to the boil, cover and simmer for 20 minutes.

3 Stir in the tofu and petit pois, and cook for a further 3 minutes. Scatter over the coriander and serve with Thai fragrant rice.

This speedy vegetarian curry has a wonderful creamy texture. Tofu, or soya bean curd, is an important source of high quality protein for vegetarians. It also provides calcium and other minerals, B and E vitamins, and antioxidants.

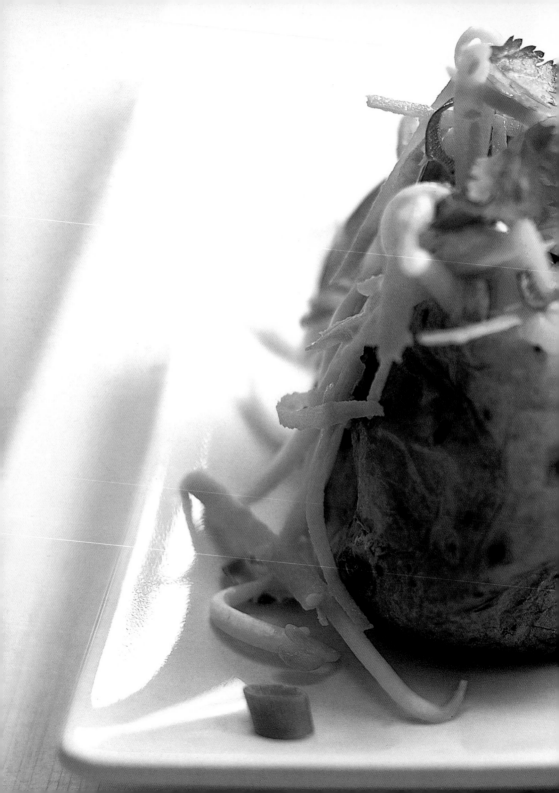

Baked jacket potatoes with oriental salad

Illustrated on previous pages

Serves 4

4 large baking potatoes, scrubbed
1 tsp olive oil
3 carrots, peeled and grated
150g (5oz) bean sprouts
4 spring onions, trimmed and
  chopped
coriander leaves, to garnish

For the dressing

1 tbsp soy sauce
2 tbsp soured cream
1 tbsp reduced-fat mayonnaise
25g (1oz) sunflower seeds, toasted
25g (1oz) sesame seeds, toasted
freshly ground black pepper

1 Preheat the oven to 200°C (fan oven 180°C), gas mark 6. Rub the baking potatoes all over with the olive oil and bake for about 1 hour until tender, turning them over halfway through cooking.

2 Meanwhile, make the dressing. In a bowl, mix together the soy sauce, soured cream, mayonnaise and toasted sunflower and sesame seeds. Season with pepper to taste.

3 Add the grated carrots, bean sprouts and chopped spring onions to the dressing and toss to mix.

4 Split the hot jacket potatoes and pile the salad on top. Garnish with coriander leaves to serve.

An excellent recipe to boost vitamin levels and contribute to your five-a-day fruit and veg.

Potato and onion cakes

Serves 4
3 medium potatoes, scrubbed
1 red onion, peeled and finely sliced
2 tbsp olive oil
freshly grated nutmeg
freshly ground black pepper

To serve
4 handfuls of baby leaf spinach
4 rashers of lean bacon, grilled
balsamic vinegar, to drizzle

1 Preheat the oven to 200°C (fan oven 180°C), gas mark 6 and put a non-stick baking tray in the oven to heat.
2 Grate the potatoes and dry well on kitchen paper. Place in a bowl, add the red onion, olive oil, a little nutmeg and black pepper, and mix well.
3 Divide the mixture into 4 portions and press into thin rounds on the hot baking tray. Bake for 25–30 minutes or until golden.
4 Arrange the spinach and grilled bacon on plates and drizzle with a little balsamic vinegar. Place the hot potato cakes on top and serve.

Onions are one of the richest sources of flavonoids – antioxidants that help our immune system.

healthy
puddings

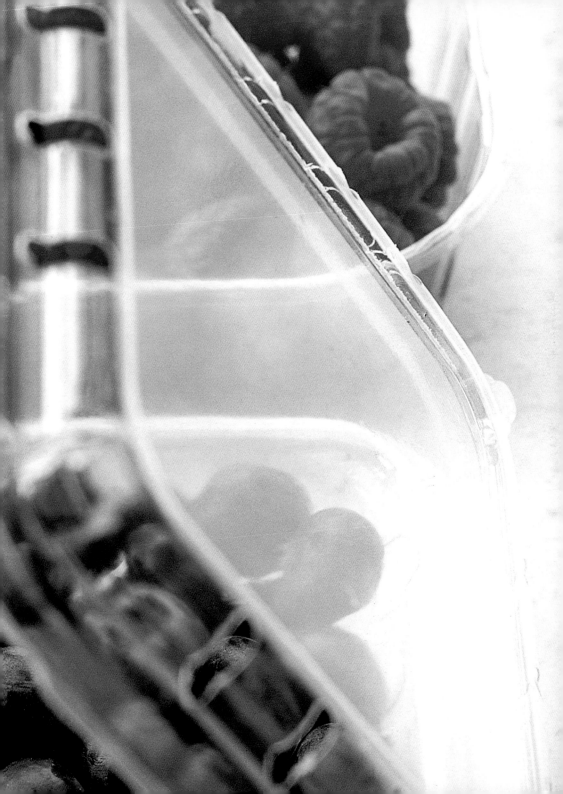

Elderflower and fruit jellies

Serves 4

7 tbsp elderflower cordial, plus extra
   to drizzle
11g sachet powdered gelatine
100g (3½oz) raspberries
100g (3½oz) blueberries

1 Dilute the elderflower cordial with 600ml (1 pint) cold water. Pour 4 tbsp into a small pan, sprinkle over the gelatine and set aside for 10 minutes.
2 Divide the raspberries and blueberries between wine glasses or tumblers.
3 Place the pan containing the softened gelatine over a very gentle heat and swirl the pan until the gelatine has completely dissolved; do not overheat. Slowly pour in the remaining diluted cordial, stirring well over a low heat.
4 Pour the elderflower jelly liquid into the glasses and chill in the refrigerator for 3 hours or until softly set. Just before serving, spoon over a little extra cordial.

This refreshing jelly, flavoured with summer berries, is a delightful way of enjoying one of your five-a-day fruit and veg. Raspberries are a particularly good source of vitamin C.

Meringue parfaits with pineapple and orange salad

Illustrated on previous pages

Serves 4

500g tub fat-free Greek yogurt

4 meringues, crumbled

65g (2½oz) blanched hazelnuts,
   toasted and chopped, plus extra to
   finish (optional)

For the fruit salad

1 small pineapple

3 large oranges

1 Line four 150ml (¼ pint) ramekins with cling film. Put the yogurt into a large bowl and gently fold in the crumbled meringues and chopped nuts. Spoon the mixture into the prepared ramekins and freeze for 2½ hours or until semi-frozen.

2 With a sharp knife, cut away the skin from the pineapple, then cut into wedges and remove the core. Cut each wedge into thin slices lengthways.

3 Using a small sharp knife, peel the oranges, removing all white pith, then cut out the segments between the membranes. Toss the pineapple slices and orange segments together in a serving bowl.

4 Turn the semi-frozen parfaits out on to serving plates and remove the cling film. Scatter with toasted chopped hazelnuts if you wish and arrange a few pieces of the fruit alongside. Serve accompanied by the rest of the pineapple and orange salad.

Crushed meringues and toasted hazelnuts are folded into creamy fat-free Greek yogurt, a good source of calcium. The mixture is semi-frozen in ramekins to make parfaits, then turned out and served with a zingy pineapple and orange salad that is rich in vitamin C.

Citrus almond cake with fruit salsa

Illustrated on previous pages

Serves 4

1 large orange, washed and
   quartered
oil, to brush tin
flour, to dust
3 eggs, beaten
50g (2oz) ground almonds
75g (3oz) instant polenta
½ tsp baking powder
125g (4oz) caster sugar
grated zest and juice of 1 lemon
icing sugar, to dust

For the fruit salsa

2 kiwi fruit, peeled
1 small, ripe mango, peeled and cut
   away from the stone
1 nectarine, halved and stoned
grated zest and juice of ½ lime

1 Place the orange in a saucepan, add enough water to cover and bring to the boil. Lower the heat and simmer for 25–30 minutes.

2 Preheat the oven to 190°C (fan oven 170°C), gas mark 5. Lightly oil and flour an 18–20cm (7–8 inch) round cake tin.

3 Remove the orange from the pan and chop roughly, discarding the pips. Put the warm chopped orange into a food processor and blend until very smooth. Add the eggs, ground almonds, polenta, baking powder, sugar and lemon zest, and whiz briefly to combine.

4 Pour the cake mixture into the prepared tin and bake for 25–30 minutes until just firm. Leave to cool in the tin slightly, then using a fork, prick the top of the cake all over and spoon over the lemon juice.

5 For the fruit salsa, chop the fruits and toss together with the lime zest and juice. Dust the cake with icing sugar and serve cut into wedges, with the fruit salsa.

Fruit salad platter with biscotti brittle

Serves 4

1 small ripe Galia melon
1 large ripe mango
2 large kiwi fruit, peeled
2 ripe nectarines, halved and stoned
225g (8oz) strawberries
100g (3½oz) biscotti biscuits
juice of 1 orange

1 Halve the melon and scoop out the seeds with a spoon, then cut away the rind. Thickly slice the melon flesh. Peel the mango and cut into chunks, slicing the flesh away from the stone. Quarter the kiwi fruit and nectarines.
2 Arrange all of the fruits attractively on a large platter. Cover with cling film and chill until ready to serve. Place the biscotti in a strong plastic bag and lightly crush with a rolling pin.
3 Just before serving, squeeze the orange juice over the chilled fruits. Scatter with the crushed biscotti and serve at once.

A fun way of enjoying more than one of your five-a-day fruit and veg. Strawberries are an exceptional source of vitamin C and high in pectin, a soluble fibre that helps reduce cholesterol levels in the body.

Pears poached in apple and cranberry juice

Serves 4

4 ripe pears, such as Red Williams
300ml (½ pint) cranberry juice
250ml (8fl oz) apple juice
finely pared zest and juice of
   ½ orange

4 cloves
1 cinnamon stick
1 rosemary sprig
50g (2oz) sugar

1 Peel the pears, retaining the stalks. Put the cranberry juice, apple juice, pared orange zest and juice, cloves, cinnamon stick, rosemary sprig and sugar in a wide saucepan. Heat gently until the sugar has dissolved.

2 Add the pear halves to the liquor and bring to the boil. Cover with a disc of greaseproof paper and reduce the heat. Poach for 30–40 minutes until the pears are tender.

3 Serve the pears warm or cold, with some of the fruity liquor. Add a dollop of fromage frais, and a little crumbled meringue if you like.

Pears at their peak of ripeness have a sublime. delicate flavour – enhanced here by poaching in fruit juice with rosemary and spices.

Chocolate and prune mousse

Illustrated on previous pages

Serves 4–6

100g (3½oz) plain dark chocolate
   (preferably luxury Belgian)
175g (6oz) ready-to-eat prunes
2 tbsp brandy (optional)
3 egg whites
1 tbsp caster sugar
cocoa powder, to dust

1 Break up the chocolate and place in a heatproof bowl over a pan of hot water. Leave until melted, then stir until smooth and leave to cool slightly.
2 Place the prunes in a saucepan and barely cover with 150ml (¼ pint) water. Simmer very gently, stirring occasionally, until very, very soft. Transfer the warm prunes and any remaining liquid to a blender or food processor, and add the brandy if using. Whiz to a smooth purée.
3 Beat the egg whites in a large clean bowl until stiff, then whisk in half of the sugar. Add the remaining sugar and beat until thick and glossy.
4 Stir the melted chocolate into the prune purée and beat together. Stir in a spoonful of the whisked egg whites to loosen the mixture, then carefully fold in the remaining egg whites.
5 Spoon the mousse into small espresso coffee cups or glasses and chill until required. Just before serving, dust with cocoa powder.

Prunes are the secret ingredient in this low-fat mousse. Like other dried fruits, they are highly nutritious and naturally sweet, so little sugar is needed. Prunes are a good source of potassium, magnesium, iron and fibre, and contain beneficial antioxidants.

Chocolate and raisin brownies

Makes 9

150g (5oz) low-fat soft cheese
140g (4½oz) muscovado sugar
40g (1½oz) cocoa powder, sifted
2 egg whites
1 tsp vanilla extract

1 tbsp semi-skimmed milk
50g (2oz) plain flour
½ tsp baking powder
75g (3oz) raisins
icing sugar, to dust

1 Preheat the oven to 180°C (fan oven 160°C), gas mark 4. Line a 15cm (6 inch) square baking tin with baking parchment.

2 In a large bowl, combine the soft cheese with the muscovado sugar. Add the cocoa powder, egg whites, vanilla extract and milk. Beat well until the mixture is smooth.

3 Sift the flour and baking powder together over the mixture, then fold in lightly, together with the raisins. Spoon the mixture into the prepared tin and bake for 25 minutes until springy to the touch.

4 Remove from the oven and allow to cool in the tin. Cut into 9 squares and dust the brownies with icing sugar just before serving.

Low-fat cream cheese and naturally sweet raisins make these brownies quite moist. They are best eaten on the day of baking, either as a dessert with yogurt, or as a treat on their own.

Apple and apricot filo pie

Serves 4

4 Cox's or small dessert apples, cored and sliced

175g (6oz) ready-to-eat dried apricots, sliced

40g (1½oz) muscovado or soft brown sugar

½ tsp ground cinnamon

grated zest of 1 lemon

squeeze of lemon juice

6 large sheets of filo pastry

2 tbsp milk

15g (½oz) butter, melted

4 tbsp thin honey

1 Preheat the oven to 190°C (fan oven 170°C), gas mark 5. Toss the apples, dried apricots, muscovado sugar, cinnamon, lemon zest and juice together in a large bowl. Set aside.

2 Fold one large sheet of filo pastry in half and lay on a non-stick baking sheet. Brush with a little milk. Cover with another folded sheet of filo and brush with milk. Scatter half of the apple and apricot mixture on top.

3 Cover with a further two sheets of folded filo, brushing each with milk, then scatter over the remaining apple mixture. Layer the remaining two sheets of filo on top, this time brushing with the melted butter.

4 Using a sharp knife, score the top layer of the pie in a diamond pattern. Bake in the oven for 40–45 minutes until the apples are cooked and the pastry is golden. Meanwhile, in a saucepan, heat the honey with 4 tbsp water and simmer for 3 minutes. Set aside to cool slightly.

5 Spoon the honey syrup over the pie and return to the oven for 5 minutes to glaze. Allow the pie to cool slightly before cutting. Serve warm with fromage frais or yogurt.

Filo is lower in fat than other pastries. Here it envelopes naturally sweet dessert apples and dried apricots to make a crisp, light pie.

Hot plum pudding

Serves 4

600g (1¼lb) plums, halved and
   stoned
finely grated zest and juice of
   1 orange
2 tbsp light muscovado sugar, plus
   extra to sprinkle
150g (5oz) plain flour

2 tsp baking powder
½ tsp ground cinnamon
40g (1½oz) caster sugar
3 tbsp milk
3 tbsp natural yogurt
1 egg
15g (½oz) butter, melted

1 Preheat the oven to 180°C (fan oven 160°C), gas mark 4. Place the plums in a shallow ovenproof serving dish in a single layer. Drizzle with the orange juice and scatter over the muscovado sugar. Bake in the oven for 15 minutes.
2 Meanwhile, sift the flour, baking powder and cinnamon together into a bowl and stir in the caster sugar. Make a well in the centre.
3 In another bowl, whisk together the milk, yogurt, egg and melted butter. Add to the dry ingredients, together with the orange zest, and mix lightly until just combined.
4 Take the baking dish from the oven and dollop the muffin mix on top of the plums, in 8 large spoonfuls to create a rough cobbler effect. Sprinkle over a little muscovado sugar.
5 Return the dish to the oven and bake for a further 20–25 minutes or until the muffin topping is golden and cooked. Serve warm with Greek yogurt, fromage frais or custard.

Hot plums nestle beneath a cinnamon-scented muffin topping in this comfort pudding, which is surprisingly low in fat and high in fibre. The topping is a cross between a crumble and a sponge.

Apple 'marmalade' with cinnamon toasts

Serves 4

4 large Cox's apples

125g (4oz) ready-to-eat dried
   apricots, sliced

grated zest and juice of 2 large
   oranges

2 tbsp dark muscovado sugar

4 cinnamon bagels

1 Halve, core and chop the apples and place in a pan with the sliced dried apricots, grated orange zest and juice, and muscovado sugar. Cook over a medium heat for 12–15 minutes until the apples are soft and jammy.

2 Split the bagels and toast lightly on both sides. Serve topped with the warm apple and apricot mixture.

An excellent recipe to boost your vitamin levels and contribute to your five-a-day fruit and veg. Serve as a warming autumnal or winter pudding, or for breakfast.

Pears with mocha fondue

Serves 4

4 ripe, firm pears

For the mocha fondue

150ml (¼ pint) semi-skimmed milk

100g (3½oz) luxury dark, bitter
   chocolate

1 tsp instant coffee

1 To make the mocha fondue, pour the milk into a pan and add the chocolate. Place over a medium heat and stir until melted.

2 Dissolve the coffee in 1 tbsp boiling water, then stir into the chocolate mixture and simmer for 2 minutes.

3 Meanwhile, quarter and core the pears, then cut into wedges. Serve the mocha sauce in espresso cups or little pots with the pear wedges for dipping.

Try varying the fruit 'dippers' – chunks of banana, whole strawberries and peach wedges are all suitable.

Apple and blackberry crunch

Serves 4
6 large Cox's apples
250g (9oz) blackberries
For the crumble
175g (6oz) plain white flour
25g (1oz) chilled butter, diced

50g (2oz) demerara sugar, plus extra
   to sprinkle
2 tbsp pumpkin seeds
2 tbsp sunflower seeds
2 tbsp orange juice

1 Preheat the oven to 200°C (fan oven 180°C), gas mark 6. Halve, core and chop the apples and place in a shallow ovenproof dish with the blackberries.
2 For the crumble, sift the flour into a bowl and rub in the butter until the mixture resembles crumbs. Stir in the demerara sugar, pumpkin and sunflower seeds and the orange juice.
3 Scatter the crumble over the fruit together with a little extra sugar. Bake for 35–40 minutes until the crumble topping is crunchy and golden. Serve with yogurt or fromage frais.

Try other combinations of fruit as they come into season, such as blackberries and apples, or peaches and raspberries.

Roasted maple fruits

Serves 4

3 small nectarines, halved and
  stoned
3 ripe pears, peeled, quartered and
  cored
3 tbsp maple syrup
3 tbsp white wine or apple juice
4 fresh figs, halved
40g (1½oz) flaked almonds

1 Preheat the oven to 200°C (fan oven 180°C), gas mark 6. Cut the nectarines
and pears into thick wedges and place in a small roasting tin.
2 Pour the maple syrup and wine or apple juice over the fruits, then toss
well to coat evenly. Roast in the oven for 10 minutes.
3 Add the figs to the roasting tin and baste with the pan juices. Scatter the
flaked almonds over the fruits and roast for a further 12–15 minutes until
the fruit is glazed and the nuts are golden. Serve hot, with yogurt or
fromage frais.

Nectarines, fresh figs and pears are roasted in
maple syrup and wine for another interesting
hot fruity dessert.

Index